Simple
PRINTMAKING

Simple
PRINTMAKING

Hand-printing projects to make at home

ELIZABETH HARBOUR

PHOTOGRAPHY BY YUKI SUGIURA • DESIGNED BY ANITA MANGAN

STACKPOLE
BOOKS

For my sister Heidi, with love x

Simple Printmaking
By Elizabeth Harbour

Published by
STACKPOLE BOOKS
5067 Ritter Road
Mechanicsburg, PA 17055
www.stackpolebooks.com

ISBN 978-0-8117-1289-7

10 9 8 7 6 5 4 3 2 1

First edition

Set in Berthold Akzidenz Grotesk and Bulmer.

Printed and bound in China.

Publisher – Alison Starling
Senior Art Editor – Juliette Norsworthy
Designer – Anita Mangan
Assistant Designer – Abigail Read
Senior Editor – Leanne Bryan
Copy Editor – Katy Denny
Proofreader – Nikki Sims
Indexer – Helen Snaith
Assistant Production Manager – Caroline Alberti
Photographer – Yuki Sugiura
Stylist – Cynthia Inions

Disclaimer

Key to project level

 easy   intermediate   difficult

CONTENTS

Introduction 6 • Printmaking basics 8

THE PROJECTS

MONO-PRINTING — 12

Technique: Creating a jelly-printing surface 14
Floral notebooks & bookmarks — 16
Bird nest wall art — 20
Flying bird mobile — 24
Love heart tote bag — 28
Home sweet home print — 31
Technique: Simple marbling — 34
Vibrant butterfly cards — 37
Pretty decorative papers — 40

STENCIL-PRINTING — 42

Children's birthday cards — 44
Summer flowers tote bag — 47
Garden birds lampshade — 50
Folk art bowls — 54

RELIEF-PRINTING — 56

Technique: Block-printing — 58
Patterned wrapping paper & tags — 60
Flying bird cushion — 62
Country house table linen — 65
Technique: Using a lino-cutting tool — 68
Dragonfly & butterfly drawer papers — 69
Autumn tablecloth — 72
Botanical curtain — 74
Feather table runner — 77
Letterheads, envelopes & tags — 80
Teatime greetings card — 82
Little boat picture — 85
Songthrush card — 88
Topiary garden print — 91

SCREEN-PRINTING — 94

Technique: Preparing your screen — 96
Hen tea towel — 99
Bluebird drawstring bag — 102
Companion cat cushion — 106
Children's party invitations — 110
Aeroplane T-shirt — 113
Butterfly-charmer scarf — 116

LITHOGRAPHY — 120

Technique: Creating a litho plate — 122
Little dog card — 124
Little fishes print — 128

Templates 132 (and inside front & back cover) • Glossary 140 • Resources 141 • Index 142 •
Acknowledgements / About the author 144

INTRODUCTION

Hand-printed cards, books, fabrics and pictures have a particular charm and are something to be treasured – especially in this age of mass-production. I am always delighted when a friend sends me a beautiful hand-printed card – it is so special and something money can't buy.

I discovered the magical world of printmaking at the age of 18 when I entered the print room of my local art college. With its huge cast-iron printing presses, hotplates warming the room and the wonderful smell of linseed oil and printing inks, this was clearly a place where alchemy happened!

Printmaking was liberating for me; it helped me to look at image-making in different ways and moved me away from a conventional approach to art. After five years of study exploring various forms of printmaking, which became key to creating some of my work, I realized that I would not have access to the wonderful college printing presses and printmaking techniques after graduation. It was then that I vowed to myself that I would find a way to create similar hand-printing techniques at home.

My dream of owning an etching press has still not been fulfilled, yet I wonder if I need one now as I think I have mastered the art of simple printmaking from home.

ABOUT THIS BOOK

This book is an introduction to various forms of printmaking, and can be used in two ways: as a handbook for printmaking processes and techniques, or as a guide to making beautiful printed objects, ranging from fabric for cushions to personalized stationery. Often people associate printmaking with prints that hang on the wall like paintings, but it can also be used to create cards, textiles, papers – all kinds of things that can surround us in our everyday lives.

Printmaking is a form of image-making using a matrix – an object on which a design has been created using one of the various printmaking processes and techniques; this is then inked up and used to make an impression to create multiples of the same image. Thus an artist's print is an original not a reproduction. Printmaking enables you to create images that cannot be made by conventional image-making. Your print matrix may take you a long time to put together, but the pay-off is that you end up with a lot more than just one finished image.

Often one of the hurdles of printmaking is the cost involved, but in this book I have

tried to think of inexpensive yet effective ways of printmaking, using products from the kitchen cupboard and acrylic paint instead of printmaking inks.

This book is rather like a recipe book that can be dipped into – and like a recipe book it has something for everyone. Often I choose the easiest recipes first and move on to more adventurous dishes when I feel confident, so feel free to use this book in a similar way.

You will find, when using some specialist products, that they might say in the small print that they can only be used in conjunction with another of that manufacturer's products. I have tried to ignore this where possible, finding cheap alternatives to keep the processes cost-effective and accessible.

ABOUT THE ARTIST

I have always been excited and fascinated by different printmaking techniques and approaches, and enjoy developing my own ways of working. As a result my work is quite diverse; this has led to me working on many different kinds of projects – and to writing this book.

I draw much of my inspiration from my home surroundings; nature and the countryside have always been fascinating to me. Every day brings something different, whether it is the swans flying across the sky or a new flower in the garden, there is always something to wonder at.

I love to make little drawings, paintings and studies. I work roughly in pencil and then with loose watercolours to work out ideas and colour combinations. Often I use tracing paper to draw on instead of plain white paper, because when I have drawn something I am happy with, it is easier to turn it over and make an accurate tracing of it and transfer it onto paper. I also love to collect things, whether it is feathers, toys, shells or stones with natural pictures on. I listen to all kinds of music and plays when I work, to get me "into the zone" or to take me to faraway places. All of these things help me to create my work.

My children are ever a source of joy and inspiration to me. My husband is wonderfully supportive, creating an inspiring environment in which I can thrive and always with a word of wisdom or humour to keep me going. Without their support I could not have made this book.

Elizabeth

PRINTMAKING BASICS

Workspace

For many of the projects I used my kitchen table (covered with a plastic tablecloth to protect it) to print on. Ideally your workspace should be a space of your own, a place at which you can dream up ideas and designs, and where you don't have to tidy away your work. The perfect space could simply be a small table with a couple of drawers for artworks to be stored safely, a jam jar with an assortment of paintbrushes and pens, a pinboard where you can keep inspirational items, an anglepoise lamp and a small plastic portfolio stored underneath to keep artwork flat and safe.

Clothing

Wear an apron or an old shirt that you don't mind getting paint on when you undertake the projects in this book to safeguard against messy accidents.

Equipment

✿ Scalpel, cutting mat and a metal ruler

Many of the projects in this book require the use of a scalpel, cutting mat and metal ruler.

A scalpel will provide many years of use and will cut very crisp lines and minimize paper tearing; it is unlike any other craft knife. It can be a little scary having to fit individual blades to the handle, but if it is treated with respect there should not be any accidents. When attaching the blade to the handle, line up the hole in the blade with the raised oval shape of metal on the handle. Slip the blade over the hole (the end of the blade should sit within the diagonal recess of the handle) then press the blade gently into a cutting mat to click it into place. Always remember to cut away from yourself when cutting and, when removing a blade, ease it off very carefully, away from your eyes. The cutting mat will protect your work surface and to some extent your blade. A metal ruler is perfect for cutting paper to size.

✿ Pencils

The three pencils mentioned in this book are grades 2B, 3B and 5H. The 2B and 3B provide

a medium dark line that won't smudge too much; they are good for most drawings. A 5H pencil is a very hard, very light pencil; it is excellent for transferring traced images, as it enables you to still see the traced image on the tracing paper once you have gone over it with the pencil – but don't press too hard with a 5H as it can create indentations on the paper.

✪ Kitchenware and utensils
For some of these projects I have used old kitchenware and utensils – pans, plates, chopping mats, baking trays, spoons and so on – that are no longer used for food preparation.

✪ Sponge and foam rollers
These items can be bought from most craft shops and range in price. A sponge roller gives a more textured paint surface, which is perfect for stencilling. A foam roller is denser and gives a more even paint surface, which is great for relief printing and lithography.

✪ Roller or brayer
This is a hard rubber roller, which is traditionally used in relief printing for rolling ink onto lino or a block. I have used this only in the relief-printing section of the book to create even pressure on the back of my block when printing.

✪ Paintbrushes
Throughout the book many of the projects use paintbrushes. For some of the projects I have used golden synthetic pointed/round paintbrushes in size 1 for fine details and size 8 for painting larger areas. The lovely thing about a size 8 brush is that it has a fatter base, which acts like an ink reservoir on a pen. This enables you to paint large areas uninterrupted and, because the brush tapers to a fine point, you can paint fine details too – it's a good all-rounder. For general paint mixing and stippling, I have used cheap round hog-hair/bristle paintbrushes and smaller brushes for manipulating paint. For applying large areas of colour, especially when mono-printing, I have used a wide hog-hair/bristle large area paintbrush. It is a good idea to have a jar of cold, clean water nearby when painting for cleaning brushes and adding water where needed. Always clean and dry your bushes after use and never leave them in water, as you will end up with bent brushes!

Materials
✪ Paint
For most of the projects in this book I have used acrylic paint (produced by recognized manufacturers of art materials), which comes in 75ml (2½fl oz) tubes. This soft-bodied water-based paint can be used on canvas, paper, wood and fabric. To keep costs to a minimum I have used the primary colours – crimson, ultramarine blue (or cobalt blue for a fresher hue) and lemon

yellow as well as black and white. These colours can be mixed to make various secondary and tertiary colours. For some of the projects I have mixed my colours 1:1 with textile medium to keep the paint "open" (it can dry very quickly) and to make it suitable for fabric printing. For other projects I have mixed in an acrylic retarder, to extend the workability of the paint. Or I have mixed it with block-printing medium to make it into relief-printing ink.

✪ Acrylic textile medium
I have used a proprietary brand of textile medium mixed with 1:1 acrylic for screen-printing and textiles. On the packaging it recommends that you use its corresponding acrylic with it; I haven't done this for quite a few of the projects yet I am very happy with the results. I recommend that you only wash the fabric "makes" in cool water, by hand.

✪ Acrylic retarder liquid
Used in certain projects to extend the drying time and workability of the paint. (Please note that both these factors can also be affected by the environment you are working in.)

✪ Fabric screen-printing ink
If you want to print and produce your own designs for retail I recommend using proper fabric screen-printing ink rather than acrylic paint. It is a lot more expensive than acrylic paint but should withstand machine washing.

✪ Paper
This can be expensive, but you get what you pay for. If you are starting out, buy cheaper paper, such as light-weight cartridge paper, sugar paper, lining paper or craft paper. If you fall in love with printmaking then look for a good supplier who will send you samples of different kinds of paper, then bulk-buy 25 sheets of a quality paper and store it flat – under a bed is ideal. Having one sheet of expensive paper is creatively stifling – having a box of lovely paper under your bed will unleash the artist within you! Paper comes in different

weights and sizes, and larger sheets can be cut down into several smaller sheets. Different papers do different things: some are very absorbent; some have a rough surface; others have a shiny hard surface. It really comes down to what you can find and the cost of it. A good-quality, heavy paper is good for cards, an absorbent paper is good for mono-prints and a smooth paper is ideal for relief-printing. Finding the right paper for a project is a matter of trial and error.

✪ Newsprint
This is unprinted newspaper that can be sourced cheaply over the Internet. Throughout the book I have used it to provide a clean work surface, and to make test prints.

✪ Photocopy paper
Useful for making paper templates for mono-printing, creating test prints and for general use.

✪ Tracing paper
Available in an A3 pad of 30 sheets, this is great for working out and transferring ideas onto paper, and also for tracing the templates in this book.

Tracing and transferring an image
Enlarge your image to the required size using a photocopier then, using tracing paper and a 3B pencil, trace over your image (a). Turn the tracing paper over so that the soft pencil lines you have just drawn are face-down on the paper, fab-foam, clear-seal backing or other surface you need to transfer a reversed design onto. Rub over the line with the blunt edge of a 5H pencil to transfer the image (b).

 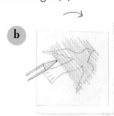

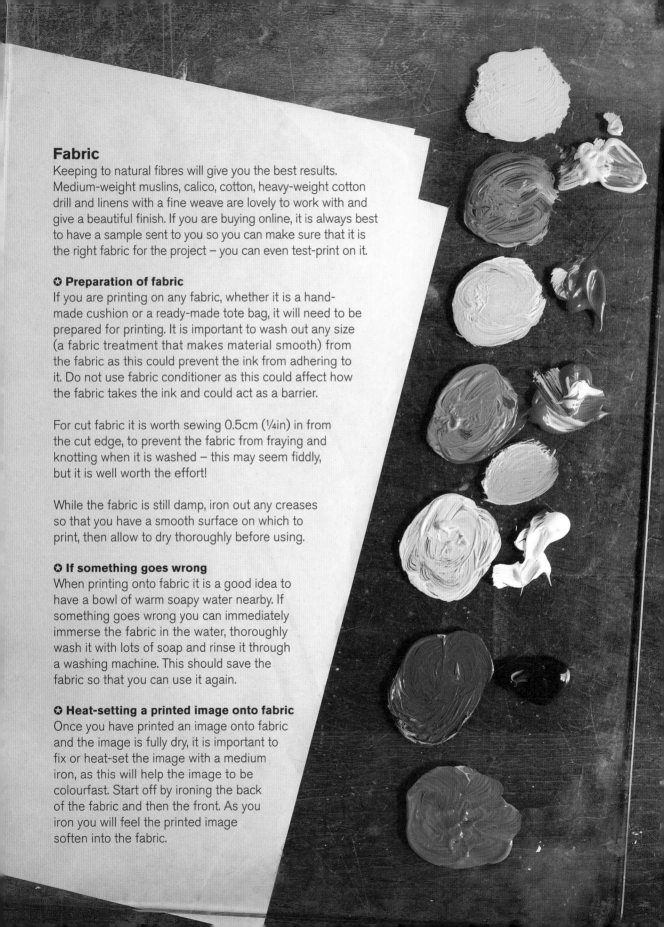

Fabric

Keeping to natural fibres will give you the best results. Medium-weight muslins, calico, cotton, heavy-weight cotton drill and linens with a fine weave are lovely to work with and give a beautiful finish. If you are buying online, it is always best to have a sample sent to you so you can make sure that it is the right fabric for the project – you can even test-print on it.

✪ Preparation of fabric

If you are printing on any fabric, whether it is a hand-made cushion or a ready-made tote bag, it will need to be prepared for printing. It is important to wash out any size (a fabric treatment that makes material smooth) from the fabric as this could prevent the ink from adhering to it. Do not use fabric conditioner as this could affect how the fabric takes the ink and could act as a barrier.

For cut fabric it is worth sewing 0.5cm (¼in) in from the cut edge, to prevent the fabric from fraying and knotting when it is washed – this may seem fiddly, but it is well worth the effort!

While the fabric is still damp, iron out any creases so that you have a smooth surface on which to print, then allow to dry thoroughly before using.

✪ If something goes wrong

When printing onto fabric it is a good idea to have a bowl of warm soapy water nearby. If something goes wrong you can immediately immerse the fabric in the water, thoroughly wash it with lots of soap and rinse it through a washing machine. This should save the fabric so that you can use it again.

✪ Heat-setting a printed image onto fabric

Once you have printed an image onto fabric and the image is fully dry, it is important to fix or heat-set the image with a medium iron, as this will help the image to be colourfast. Start off by ironing the back of the fabric and then the front. As you iron you will feel the printed image soften into the fabric.

MONO-PRINTING

Mono-printing is often referred to as a printed painting. It is a spontaneous and playful way of image-making. No two prints are the same; each will have subtle differences and variations. This printing process offers all kinds of possibilities for image-making – the chance to move and manipulate paint, to make collages from images and create layers within an image.

Whenever I create mono-prints there is one thought that always pops into my head while I print: "I wonder what will happen if I do this?". You have to keep an eye on what you are doing, as there are some wonderful surprises on the way to achieving a print. Whether it is an accident or something that has happened while you are focusing on something else, you will find that all sorts of images appear in the process of making a print. Remember these moments as they will provide inspiration in the future.

I discovered jelly-printing relatively late in life. I had thought that really detailed mono-prints could be achieved only with an etching press. But this sort of detail is also achievable with jelly-printing, with its soft wipeable printing surface and flexibility of where it can be used.

Marbling is another fun mono-printing technique, and one that is particularly good to get kids involved with. It takes a little patience to set everything up but the results are simply stunning.

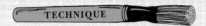

CREATING A JELLY-PRINTING SURFACE

GELATINE SURFACE

150g (5oz) powdered gelatine (I used 2 x 65g/2½oz boxes) – do not use leaf gelatine

Deep saucepan

400ml (14fl oz) cold water

400ml (14fl oz) boiling-hot water

Whisk

25 x 35cm (10 x 14in) nonstick Swiss roll or brownie baking tin, approx. 3cm (1¼in) deep

Knife

Chopping mat or old chopping board

Kitchen paper

Clingfilm

Old heavy saucepan

METHOD

1. Mix the gelatine

Pour the powdered gelatine into a deep saucepan; add the cold water and stir well. The gelatine will be very thick and lumpy at this point. Add the boiling-hot water, then whisk gently over a low heat until the gelatine powder has dissolved.

2. Set the gelatine

Place the baking tin on a level surface, then pour the gelatine mixture into the tin and allow it to set in a cool place. (Normally I allow the gelatine to set in a cool room, as once it is set it is the perfect temperature for printing. If your house is very warm you may need to set your gelatine in the fridge.)

3. Prepare the gelatine for printing

Once the gelatine is thoroughly set, it should be very firm and relatively easy to handle. Gently tease it out of the tin with a knife with one hand underneath for support (and to prevent it from cracking), and turn it over onto a chopping mat or old chopping board so that the smooth side faces upwards. If you have stored your gelatine in the fridge, allow the gelatine to reach room temperature for an hour before printing. (If it is too cold the surface will become damp, resulting in watery prints and loss of definition.)

If you are doing a series of prints in the the same or similar colours, the jelly surface won't need to be cleaned between colours. However if you change from using a dark colour to a light colour, the surface will need cleaning as there will be some residue paint left on it, which could darken a lighter colour. To clean the surface, gently wipe it with damp kitchen paper.

4. Using your gelatine again

Once you have finished printing, wash the paint off the gelatine with cold water. Don't worry if the gelatine breaks up; drain off any water and place the pieces in an old heavy saucepan that is no longer used for food. Melt it over a gentle heat, but do not boil it. Pour the liquid gelatine back into the baking tin and allow it to set. Once it has set, tease it out of the tin and place it on a plastic chopping mat. Place another plastic chopping mat on top of it and wrap it with clingfilm. The gelatine will keep in the fridge for at least a couple of weeks, so that you can use it for more mono-printing.

FLORAL NOTEBOOKS & BOOKMARKS
jelly-printing – ghost prints

This project is a wonderful introduction to the delights of mono-printing. Floral mono-prints are a magical and immediate way of printing that can be enjoyed by all the family, and it's relatively easy to produce stunning results. The types of flowers and foliage available through the seasons will produce different kinds of images, and furnish you with a wealth of ideas for colours.

YOU WILL NEED

Newspaper or wipeable tablecloth

Soft, pliable paper (try selection of different kinds of paper to see which gives the best results)

Soft-bodied acrylic paint – crimson, ultramarine blue, lemon yellow and white

3 round-headed bristle paintbrushes

Acrylic retarder liquid

A jar of cold water

Old plate or chopping mat, for mixing paints

Sponge roller

Prepared gelatine surface (see page 14)

Flowers, foliage, ferns and seasonal flowers (avoid anything woody, thick and hard-stemmed as this will pierce the gelatine and spoil the printing surface)

Newsprint or other scrap paper

Tweezers

Notebooks (the type with a plain cover, creamy paper inside and two staples in the gutter is perfect)

Craft knife

Metal ruler

Cutting mat

PVA glue

5cm (2in) decorator's brush or wide, hog-hair paintbrush

For the bookmarks

Thick card

Hole punch

Coloured ribbon

LEVEL
Easy

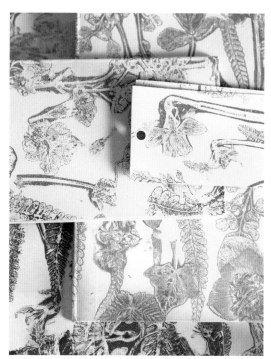

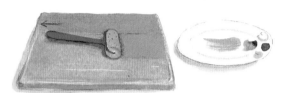

METHOD

1. Prepare your paper and workspace

Work in a cool space on a clear, level work surface –
a kitchen table covered in newspaper or a wipeable
tablecloth would work well. If you have large sheets
of paper, cut them to approximately 2.5cm (1in) larger
than the gelatine surface.

2. Mix the paint colours

The colours I mixed are:

Lime green – from white, yellow and a little blue
Pink – from crimson, white and a little yellow
Lilac – from white, blue and a little crimson

When mixing the colours for printing, the consistency
should be easy enough for the brush to pass through. If it is
too stiff or too watery you will not achieve definition in your
prints. Add a little retarder, using the tip of a paintbrush, to
prevent the acrylic from drying too quickly, and a little water,
if necessary, to achieve the right consistency. Don't work
under a direct warm spotlight, as this will hasten the drying
process and hence affect the workability of the paint.

3. Prepare the gelatine

Once you have achieved the correct paint consistency,
roll your sponge roller in the paint and then roll the paint
onto the surface of the gelatine. Cover the entire surface
with paint, reloading the roller as you go, until you have
a thin, even layer of paint **(a)**. Try to work speedily to
prevent the paint from drying out.

4. Arrange the flowers and foliage

Gently place your flower heads and foliage onto the
painted surface **(b)**, taking care not to disturb the painted
surface by moving the foliage or transferring fingerprints.

5. Take a silhouette print

Take a piece of newsprint and lay it over the flowers.
Gently smooth down the paper, feeling around the
flowers and foliage with your fingertips, applying a light
pressure over the whole surface of the paper. Carefully
lift the paper off. You should have a silhouette print of the
flowers and foliage. Working speedily to avoid the paint
drying out before you take your print, carefully remove the
foliage and flowers from the surface of the gelatine using
tweezers. You will see, as you remove the greenery, that
there is an impression of the foliage and flowers in the
paint **(c)** – a ghost print. Be careful not to smudge this.

6. Take your print – the ghost print

Once you have removed all the greenery, lay your printing
paper smooth side down onto the gelatine surface **(d)**.
Taking care not to move the paper, smooth over the whole
surface of the paper firmly with the palm of your hand.
Gently lift the paper off the gelatine and you should have
a lovely flower print!

7. Prepare to cover your notebooks

Once your printed papers have dried, you can use them
to cover your notebooks. First of all, take a notebook
and work out where to position it on the reverse side

of a sheet of printed paper, making sure that the borders are the same width on all sides and that the whole of the notebook's cover will be covered with the printed image. You may need to trim your paper a little to do this.

8. Glue the front

Place a sheet of newsprint or scrap paper between the front cover and the first page of your notebook to prevent the cover from sticking to the first page once you've glued on the printed paper. Mix a little water into some PVA glue to make it easier to brush on. Brush the glue quickly and evenly onto the front cover of your notebook. Place the glued cover of your notebook onto the reverse side of your printed paper. Lift up the interior of the book and press down onto the inside of the front cover with the palm of your hand.

9. Glue the back

Place another sheet of newsprint between the back cover and the last page of your notebook. Apply a little glue to the spine and back cover of the book. Lift the front cover of your book and press down the book's spine onto the paper. Place the glued back cover down on the reverse side of the printed-paper, (try to keep the paper fairly tight as it may end up baggy or creased). Press down onto the inside of the back cover with the palm of your hand.

10. Finish the books

Depending on the type of book you are covering, the paper can either be trimmed flush to the cover's edge or folded over the cover's edge and glued. Folding over is slightly trickier as you will need to lift the top spine of the book and glue the edge of the paper underneath this, and trim the cover's corners before gluing the sides.

11. Making bookmarks

Make bookmarks by gluing the flower-printed paper onto thick card. Once it is dry, cut it into strips roughly 6.5 x 15cm (2^2/$_3$ x 6in) to make bookmarks. To finish the bookmarks punch a hole centrally in the top edge of each and thread with a coloured ribbon.

BIRD NEST WALL ART
jelly-printing – manipulated paint, layers & collage

This project shows how you can layer various mono-printed effects to create a more interesting image. The design is composed of manipulated paint and textures, and uses stencils.

Once you get the hang of this technique you can introduce more elements, such as flower prints and printed textures to create larger, more exciting images. It is always worth sourcing a good-quality paper for making prints, as you may want to frame them.

TIP

When cutting the gelatine to size for this make, keep the off-cuts as these can be melted down along with the cleaned gelatine printing surface after printing, to create a new printing surface.

YOU WILL NEED

Prepared gelatine surface (see page 14)

Sharp knife

Tracing paper

2B pencil

5H pencil

Light-weight cartridge paper or white copier paper

Scalpel (X-Acto knife) fitted with 10A blade, or craft knife

Masking tape

Cartridge paper or other good-quality paper, cut to correct size for picture frame, a little larger than your gelatine (25 x 22cm/10 x 8½in).

Soft-bodied acrylic paint – crimson, ultramarine blue, lemon yellow, black and white

3 round-headed bristle paintbrushes

Acrylic retarder liquid

A jar of cold water

Old plate or chopping mat, for mixing paints

5cm (2in) decorator's brush or wide, hog-hair paintbrush

A size 1 fine, pointed, round paintbrush

LEVEL

Intermediate

TEMPLATES

Bird and eggs (see inside front cover), enlarged by 141%

METHOD

1. Prepare the gelatine surface and template

Cut the gelatine with a sharp knife to 20 x 16.5cm (8 x 6⅓in). Enlarge the Bird and eggs template on the inside front cover, then trace and transfer the outline onto light-weight cartridge paper (see page 10). Cut out the bird and eggs using a scalpel or craft knife on a cutting mat. (Remember that this is a template and not a stencil – you will be using the bird and eggs shapes rather than the surrounding paper, not vice versa.)

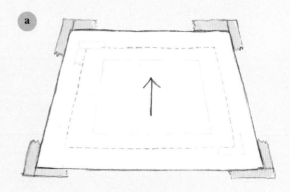

2. Create registration marks for your print

In order to ensure the multiple layers print in the correct place you can use masking tape to create registration marks to guide you. Stick tape on the table around the edges of the cutting mat or old chopping board on which the gelatine surface is sitting, so that it doesn't move out of place while you are printing. Then take the paper to be printed on and, with a pencil, draw an arrow on the back to show which way round it should be when printing. Lightly lay the paper (the right way up) onto the gelatine so that it is centrally placed under the paper. Place tape on the table where the four corners of the paper fall **(a)**. When you come to print, if you make sure that the paper is the right way up and sits within the four masked corners you should have a registered print.

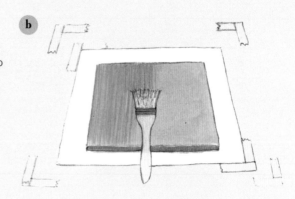

3. Print the first background layer

Mix crimson paint with white and a little yellow to make a warm pink colour. Mix the paint together with a small amount of acrylic retarder liquid, to prevent the acrylic from drying out, and a little water, if necessary, to achieve the right consistency. Paint the gelatine surface with a decorator's brush or a wide, hog-hair paintbrush using vertical strokes so that the surface is streaked with paint **(b)**. Place the paper onto the painted surface being careful to line the corners up with the registration marks, and with the pencil arrow pointing the right way. Smooth evenly over the whole gelatine surface with the palm of your hand. Remove the paper.

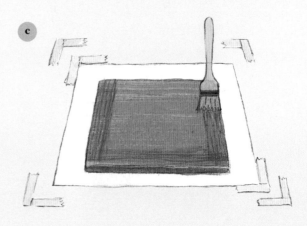

4. Print the second background layer

Mix white, blue and a little crimson paint with a small amount of retarder and water, if necessary, to make a pale lilac colour. Paint the gelatine surface again with warm pink, this time with horizontal brush strokes. Using a little of the lilac, paint around the edge of the gelatine surface with a wider, streaky strip of paint to create a soft frame of colour **(c)**. Again, position your first print within the masking tape registration marks and print the image, again smoothing evenly over the whole gelatine surface with the palm of your hand. Remove the paper. At this point don't worry if there is a little mis-registration; this can add another dimension to the overall look of the print.

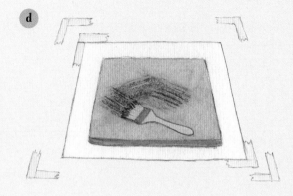

5. Prepare the third layer

Mix a little black, blue and white paint to create a blue-black colour. Again, add a small amount of retarder and a little water, if necessary. Paint a circular nest shape in the centre of the gelatine surface using feathered semi-circular movements of the brush **(d)**. Make sure that the nest is big enough so that the bird and eggs templates will be framed within it.

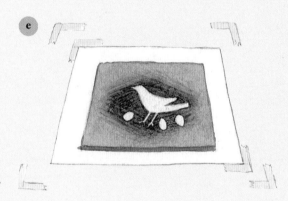

6. Print the third layer

Place the bird and eggs templates on top of the nest **(e)**. Take care not to disturb the painted surface. Reposition the paper onto the gelatine within the registration marks, and gently smooth over the whole of the surface with the palm of your hand paying particular attention to where the birds and eggs are positioned. The bird and egg templates will act as mask so that the cross-hatched pink surface will show through. Remove the print and, with the small, fine brush and a little blue-black paint, dot a small eye directly onto the mono-printed bird. Allow to dry and then frame your print.

FLYING BIRD MOBILE
jelly-printing – mono-printed textures & patterns

Before my daughter was born I made her a mobile of little hand-painted animals. When she became a teenager I decided that it was time to make her a new one.

There are many birds in our garden because of the majestic trees that surround the house. I thought that it would be interesting to create something that reflected their flying forms by employing unusual mono-printed patterns, textures and colour combinations. The printing techniques described here, which manipulate paint on the printing surface in different ways to create different printed effects, work beautifully to create a flying bird mobile.

TIP

The lace I have used is quite deep. If your lace is narrow, cut a few long strips and lay them together on the painted gelatine.

YOU WILL NEED

Tracing paper

3B pencil

5H pencil

A2-sized sheet of heavy-weight cartridge paper

Scalpel (X-Acto knife) fitted with 10A blade, or craft knife

Cutting mat

Bradawl

Soft-bodied acrylic paint – crimson, ultramarine blue, lemon yellow, black and white

5 round-headed bristle paintbrushes

Acrylic retarder liquid

A jar of cold water

Old plate or chopping mat, for mixing paints

Prepared gelatine surface (see page 14)

5cm (2in) decorator's brush or wide, hog-hair paintbrush

Newsprint

Cotton lace with open design

A size 5 or medium pointed, round paintbrush

Bubble wrap

For the mobile

1mm hole punch (optional)

4 x 35cm (14in) pieces of 6mm (¼in) wooden dowel or baton, painted to desired colour

Linen cord or thin string

Scissors

Nylon beading thread

LEVEL

Intermediate

TEMPLATES

Flying birds (see inside back cover), enlarged by 141%

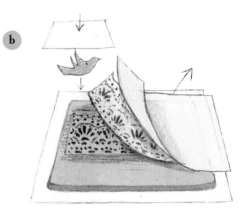

METHOD

1. Prepare the birds

Enlarge the Flying birds templates on the inside back cover, then trace and transfer the outlines onto heavy cartridge paper (see page 10), and carefully cut them out using a scalpel or craft knife on a cutting mat. You need 40 birds; you can either use all eight templates or choose your favourites (I made five birds in each of the eight designs). Using the bradawl, make holes in the birds where the dots are marked – these are for threading with nylon thread later.

2. Mix the paint colours

I have used various colours for the birds, working with one colour at a time. Choose from the following:

Purple – crimson, ultramarine blue and a little white
Dark purple – add a touch of black and a little more ultramarine blue into the purple mix
Pink – crimson and white
Warm pink – add a little lemon yellow into the pink mix
Green – ultramarine blue, lemon yellow and white
Pale green – add more white into the green mix
Blue green – add more ultramarine blue into the green mix
Lavender blue – blue, white and a little crimson

Add a little retarder to each colour to prevent the acrylic from drying too quickly, and a little water, if necessary; also don't work directly under a warm spotlight, as this will hasten the drying and hence the workability of the paint.

3. Print the horizontal streaked birds

Using a decorator's brush or a wide, hog-hair paintbrush and pink paint, paint horizontal streaks onto the gelatine surface **(a)**. Lay two or three bird templates onto the painted gelatine and place newsprint over the top. Gently press down onto the surface with the palm of your hand. Repeat this process for the other sides of the birds. You will find, as you print the birds, that the newsprint will have silhouetted images of birds printed on it, which is rather pretty. If you like, you could try using better paper to capture the results. And if you use the same sheet several times, you could get some very interesting random images.

4. Print the cross-hatched birds

Using another colour, for example purple, paint vertical streaks of paint onto the gelatine surface. Take some of the pink printed birds and lay them down onto the gelatine so that the brush strokes are at a right angle to the previous horizontal strokes printed on them. Lay newsprint over the birds and press gently. Repeat this on the other side of each bird.

5. Print the lace birds

Paint the surface of the gelatine in dark purple paint with vertical or horizontal strokes – it doesn't really matter as long as they are all in the same direction. Lay the lace down onto the printed surface and take a silhouette print using newsprint, pressing gently with the palm of your hand. Gently lift the lace off – you should have a

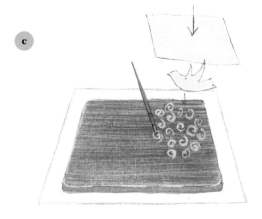

detailed lace impression on the gelatine. Next lay one or more birds onto one half of the lace impression so that you can print on the other half to keep continuity of colour and pattern. Lay a small piece of newsprint over the birds, taking care not to disturb the other half of the lace impression **(b)**. Gently smooth over the newsprint with the palm of your hand. Lift up the newsprint and birds, which should have a detailed image of lace printed upon them. Print the other side of the birds on the other section of the lace impression. You can print on top of some of the pink printed birds to create more depth of colour.

6. Print the manipulated paint birds

Paint the gelatine surface with purple paint using horizontal strokes. Using a clean, fine paintbrush, make spiral patterns in the surface of the gelatine, cleaning the paint from the paintbrush as you go. Again try to use one half of the painted gelatine to print a few birds **(c)**. Print the other side of the birds using the other half of the gelatine surface.

7. Print the bubble wrap texture birds

Paint the gelatine with lavender blue paint using horizontal brush strokes. Place the bubble wrap onto the gelatine, bubble side down; press down with the palm of your hand then carefully peel the bubble wrap off the gelatine. An impression of bubble wrap should be left upon the painted surface. Again, try to use one half of the painted gelatine to print a few birds, then print the other side of the birds

using the other half of the gelatine surface. The bubble wrap will now have lavender blue paint on it; if you like, you could print it on top of some of the birds you printed earlier to create more depth of colour. Alternately, you could paint your gelatine surface with another paler colour and place the unwiped bubble wrap onto the painted surface; the colour from the bubble wrap will transfer to the surface creating circles in a different colour to the background. This can be printed from. If you want to achieve another clean bubble-wrap impression, just wipe the paint off the wrap and repeat the original process. Allow all the printed birds to dry.

8. Make the mobile

If you wish, use a 1mm hole punch to punch out the eyes of the birds. Arrange the four painted wooden batons in a square, overlaying them at each corner. Lash the batons together at each corner with the cord or string to make a square frame. Tie a 50cm (20in) length of cord or string from each corner. Bring the ends of the cord together **(d)**, check that the wooden frame hangs level, and tie the cords into a knot. Hang the mobile frame low and level from the ceiling so that you can reach it to hang the birds on. Thread the birds with beading thread, knotting to secure. Arrange and tie at varying lengths along the wooden batons, affixing 10 birds to each baton, and trim the tied ends of cord or string to neaten.

LOVE HEART TOTE BAG
jelly-printing – mono-printed ghost print on fabric

This delightful tote bag captures the beauty of summer flowers and is an example of how you can successfully capture delicate mono-printed details on fabric. It makes a unique and lovely birthday gift or Mother's Day present.

The image could also be printed onto a cushion, laundry bag, pillowcase or paper to make a lovely print for a bedroom. You could even make a smaller heart template to use for a Valentine's Day card or lavender bags.

It is best to use a neutral-coloured fabric with a fine weave, as it will pick up all the small details and help these to stand out. Calico, cotton and medium-weight muslin work particularly well for this printing technique and are very reasonably priced.

YOU WILL NEED

Cotton tote bags

Steam iron and ironing board

A3 sheet of tracing paper

3B pencil

5H pencil

A3 sheet cartridge paper

Scalpel (X-Acto knife) fitted with 10A blade, or craft knife

Cutting mat

Soft-bodied acrylic paint – crimson, blue and white

A round-headed bristle paintbrush

Acrylic textile medium

A jar of cold water

Old plate or chopping mat, for mixing paints

Newsprint

Prepared gelatine surface (see page 14)

5cm (2in) decorator's brush or wide, hog-hair paintbrush

A selection of flower heads

Tweezers

LEVEL
Easy

TEMPLATE
Love heart (see inside front cover), enlarged by 141%

METHOD

1. Prepare the bags
First wash the tote bags to wash out any size in the fabric (see page 11). Allow to dry and iron with a hot steam iron.

2. Prepare the heart template
Enlarge the Love heart template on the inside front cover, making sure that it is just the right size to fit within your gelatine printing surface, then trace and transfer the outline centrally onto the cartridge paper (see page 10). Cut out the heart using a scalpel or craft knife on a cutting mat. Discard the heart shape and retain the surrounding paper.

3. Mix the paint colours
Mix blue and crimson paint with a little white to make a lavender blue, then add a similar volume of acrylic textile

medium to the paint, and a little water if needed. Mix thoroughly. Don't work under a direct warm spotlight, as this will hasten the drying process and hence affect the workability of the paint. Place a sheet of newsprint into each bag to prevent any paint seeping through the fabric when you print.

4. Prepare the printing surface

Place the gelatine printing surface in a portrait position and paint the surface evenly with vertical strokes using the decorator's brush or hog-hair paintbrush (this leaves a little residue on the ghost print, creating a stronger image). Arrange a selection of flower heads into a rough heart shape. Hold the heart stencil upside down above the flowers to make sure that it will be filled with flower heads **(a)**. The heart is upside down so that the handles of the bag will hang clear off the table and won't get in the way during printing.

5. Get ready to print

Lay a piece of newsprint over the flower heads to take your first silhouette print. Gently smooth over the newsprint with the palm of your hand. Take the paper off and gently remove the flower heads using tweezers – you should be able to see a good flower impression on the gelatine. If it isn't clear enough paint the surface again with a little more paint and repeat the process. It is advisable to take a paper print to check to see if everything is working in the right way. When it looks as if you have a good flower impression on the gelatine, place the heart template upside down onto the surface so that the negative heart shape is filled with flower impressions **(b)**. It is important to cover any remaining painted surfaces with strips of paper to prevent any unwanted paint getting onto the bag.

6. Print the bag

Hold the first tote bag upside down over the heart template, positioning it so that the heart image will be centrally positioned on the bag once it is printed (I allowed about 7.5cm (3in) from the bottom of the bag). Place the bag down onto the printing surface and smooth the fabric with the palm of a clean hand **(c)**. You should be able to feel the outline of the template and apply pressure where

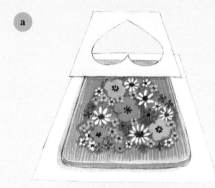

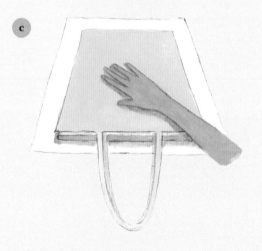

the printed image will be. Gently lift the opening of the bag without moving the fabric and smooth over the inner paper. Carefully lift one corner of the bag and gently remove from the gelatine surface. Hang to dry and, once it is dry, brush off any seeds or stamens and heat-set the printed fabric with a medium iron (see page 11).

HOME SWEET HOME PRINT
jelly-printing – collaged mono-printing

This little print embodies my love for samplers and folk art. The project is a very enjoyable way of composing images, and is achieved by arranging elements as in a collage and then printing from them. A further fun element is seeking out foliage and leaves that look like miniature trees.

It is worth looking out for and collecting different kinds of lace and anything that you think would print well, especially haberdashery trimmings, punched paper designs and intricate doilies. This project would make a lovely moving house gift or card.

YOU WILL NEED

Sharp knife

Prepared gelatine surface (see page 14)

Scalpel (X-Acto knife) fitted with 10A blade, or craft knife

Tracing paper

3B pencil

5H pencil

White copier paper

Cutting mat

Soft-bodied acrylic paint – crimson, ultramarine blue and white

A round-headed bristle paintbrush

A jar of cold water

Acrylic retarder liquid

Old plate or chopping mat, for mixing paints

5cm (2in) decorator's brush or wide, hog-hair paintbrush

Scissors

Flowers, plus foliage and ferns that resemble little trees and bushes (avoid anything woody, thick and hard-stemmed as this will pierce the gelatine and spoil the printing surface

Lace ribbon of varying widths with an open design

Tweezers

Soft, pliable white/cream paper for printing

LEVEL
Easy

TEMPLATE
House (see inside back cover)

a b c

METHOD

1. Prepare surface and templates

Cut the gelatine surface with a sharp knife to 16 x 11cm (6¼ x 4¼in). Trace the House template on the inside back cover, then transfer the outline onto white copier paper (see page 10), and cut it out carefully using a scalpel or craft knife on a cutting mat. (It is worth cutting out several templates so that you can make a few prints.) Cut lengths of lace ribbon to make a frame around the edge of the gelatine surface.

2. Mix the paint colours

Mix ultramarine blue with a small amount of crimson and white paint to make lavender blue. Add a little retarder and a little more water than usual so that the brush moves easily through the paint – the paint must not be too wet, but it should leave a residue on the gelatine after the silhouette print is taken. (The best way to gauge the right consistency is to take some test prints with small bits of foliage and small scraps of paper.)

3. Apply paint and templates

Using a decorator's brush or a wide, hog-hair paintbrush, carefully paint the gelatine surface with horizontal brushstrokes, making sure that the strokes are close together. Arrange strips of lace ribbon around the edges of the gelatine to make a border, using a deeper lace for the bottom edge to represent the landscape in the foreground. Position the little house centrally on the bottom border of the lace ribbon **(a)**.

4. Place the foliage

Select leaves and foliage that look like trees, pulling off a few leaves at the base of sprigs and leaves to create the trunk of a tree **(b)**. Position these on the bottom border of the lace ribbon to create a scene. I placed a daisy head face down on the gelatine (remember that your image will print back to front!) to represent the sun.

5. Take a silhouette print

Place a sheet of white copier paper over the gelatine and smooth gently over the back of the paper with the palm of your hand. (Don't press too hard as this will transfer all the paint to the silhouette print – we need some residue paint to be left as this helps to define the outline of the little house.) Remove the paper and you should have a rather nice silhouette print, which could be trimmed and mounted to make another picture.

6. Print the picture

With tweezers carefully remove the lace and foliage from the gelatine, but not the house template as this will act as a stencil **(c)**. You should be able to see an impression of the lace and foliage on the gelatine surface. Place your printing paper centrally over the image, so that it will have an evenly sized white border, and smooth firmly with the palm of your hand. Remove the print paper and allow it to dry. This picture looks lovely in a simple pale grey or limed frame and makes a great moving house gift.

SIMPLE MARBLING

One summer I bought my children a marbling kit. They spent hours floating and manipulating inks on the marbling bath surface, creating numerous sheets of pretty papers. Marbling is a magical form of mono-printing, perfect for children as they are so experimental and full of fresh ideas.

My only regret that summer was that I had to meter the use of the marbling ink as we had only small pots of it. This got me thinking – if marbling inks are made from liquid acrylic then surely one could make one's own out of acrylic paints? My solution was carrageenan, which works with watered-down acrylics. It is non-toxic and can be bought easily via the Internet.

I have tried to keep the costs and preparation time down for this section. If you want to take marbling further you can buy Alum (potassium aluminum sulphate) to treat papers and fabrics before marbling to help the marbling adhere to surfaces. Marbling inks are also available.

MARBLING KIT

Marbling trays – these should be clear, white or pale in colour so that the marbling inks are visible on the surface. If you want to start off small, a (new) cat-litter tray, washing-up bowl or foil tray are good for making cards and tags. For marbling large sheets of paper, clear shallow plastic under-bed storage boxes are perfect

Measuring jug

Clean bucket, for making up large quantities of size

Teaspoon

Carrageenan

Dust mask

Warm tap water – if you find that your paints are not floating properly, use purified water

Old hand-whisk

Soft-bodied acrylic paint – crimson, cobalt or ultramarine blue, lemon yellow, black, white, or even bronze

Several old or cheap paintbrushes, for mixing colours

Distilled or de-ionised water, for thinning down acrylics

5–10 small jam jars with lids, for mixing paints

Apron or old clothes

Plastic gloves

Pasteur pipettes – have a pipette for each colour; if you do not have enough pipettes, clean the pipette out between colours by filling and expelling with water

Clean stick or the end of a paintbrush

Paper or card – most types work well; it really comes down to trial and error, and availability. Coloured paper can be very effective providing a contrasting background to the marbling. Some papers can be too absorbent: for these papers keep their size small and work quickly

Water bath – the same size as your marbling tray

Washing line with pegs or a clothes airer with plastic-covered bars (which can be wiped clean after use)

Iron and ironing board

For the combs

Cardboard box

Scissors

Cocktail sticks or kebab skewers

Glue

Reinforcing card or thick paper

When to marble

It is best to marble on a warm, windless sunny day as this kind of weather helps to set and dry the marbled papers. If you are marbling large sheets of paper it is best to marble outside or in a utility room with a washable floor and easy access to the outside. Marbling can be messy and wet and can create slippery floors, especially if you are marbling large papers. To minimize this allow the marbling size (water thickened with carrageenan) to drip off the paper before transporting the paper to the water bath.

1. Prepare your marbling bath

Do a weather check and prepare the marbling bath 6–12 hours ahead of marbling, ideally the night before you want to marble. Place the marbling tray on a protected, level surface, before you fill it. The size of your tray will determine how much marbling size you will need to prepare. To work out how much size you need to make up a marbling bath of any size, measure how much water is needed to fill the tray to a depth of 5cm (2in) (do this outside and tip the water away) then use a dry teaspoon to measure out 2 tsp carrageenan for every 1 litre (1¾ pints) warm tap water. (Warning: do not breathe in the carrageenan while you are preparing the solution; either wear a dust mask or mix it in a well-ventilated, non-breezy area.) To fill a standard washing-up bowl, mix up 2 litres (3½ pints) of marbling size. You will find that the carrageenan will clump together, so whisk the mixture at this stage to break up any lumps, and periodically to help it to dissolve. After 6–12 hours it will be ready. The size should last for two to three days.

2. Prepare the marbling inks

Squeeze out a blob of acrylic paint, add it to three parts distilled or de-ionised water and mix thoroughly. If the ink is too watery, it will disperse across the marbling bath so that it is very faint; if it is too thick, it will sink to the bottom of the bath. It is best to add a little water at a time and to test the ink in the marbling bath until you are satisfied with its consistency.

3. Mix the colours

Warm red – crimson and yellow
Lemon yellow
Ultramarine blue
Light blue – white and cobalt blue
Pink – crimson and white
Lilac – crimson, cobalt blue and white
Lime green – cobalt blue, yellow and white
Grey – black and white

4. Make a marbling comb

It is useful to have a variety of different marbling combs with varied spacing between the teeth; it's good to start with two combs, one of 1cm (½in) and one of 2cm (¾in).

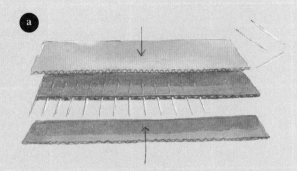

If you have a square marbling bath you will need only one comb of each size, but if you have a rectangular one you will need to make two combs: one that fits the length of the tray comfortably and one that fits the width.

The type of cardboard box you have will determine whether you will need to use cocktail sticks or kebab skewers for your comb's teeth. You should find, when the card is cut, that it has channels running through it. Smaller channels are perfect for cocktail sticks; larger channels are more suited to kebab skewers. From a box, cut a strip of cardboard that is 5cm (2in) wide and as long as the width of the marbling bath. Make sure that you cut the cardboard so its channels span the width of the card. If the cardboard is not long enough stick two pieces together. Position sticks firmly into the channels, spacing them evenly like the teeth of a comb. Glue and mount the back of the card to a long reinforcing strip of card or thick paper. Glue another strip of reinforcing card on top, so that the comb is sandwiched in between the two, and allow to dry **(a)**.

5. Prepare your workspace

Before you embark on the marbling process:
– Arrange the colours next to the marbling bath.
– Place clothes pegs at evenly spaced intervals on the washing line.
– Wear old clothes or protect your clothing with an apron. Protect your hands with plastic gloves.
– Position your water bath close by, for rinsing the paper. (I tend to have mine on the floor outside, as it is easier to empty – it is really down to whatever suits you.)
– Prepare your paper – trim or cut it to fit the size of the marbling bath.
– Store your paper in a dry area.

VIBRANT BUTTERFLY CARDS
basic marbling

After spending hours of fun with my two children marbling beautiful little sheets of paper, I wondered what to do with them. With a little imagination marbled papers can be turned into these gorgeous little cards!

YOU WILL NEED

Marbling kit (see page 34)

Medium- to heavy-weight paper (that will stand when folded), trimmed to fit easily into the marbling bath

Tracing paper

3B pencil

5H pencil

Scalpel (X-Acto knife) fitted with 10A blade, or craft knife

Cutting mat

LEVEL

Easy

TEMPLATES

Butterflies (see inside front cover), enlarged by 141%, or to fit within the size of your cards

METHOD

1. Add colour to the marbling bath

Using a pipette suck up the selected colour and, holding the end over the marbling bath release droplets onto the liquid surface. (Use a paintbrush to sprinkle droplets of colour if you don't own a pipette.) Experiment by dropping and swirling colours. Start off by gently swirling the colours with the end of a paintbrush or by making little circular movements. You will notice, when using the pipettes, that you can be very controlled in releasing the drops of colour so that they can be evenly spaced **(a)**. You can also drop other colours one at a time within the first droplets of colour to create concentric circles of colour. You may notice that some of the colours you are using float and spread more successfully than others. Some colours may prevent other colours dispersing properly (often colours with white in, so it is best to put these in last). If a colour is really problematic add a little white to it and mix it in thoroughly; even though this lightens the colour it helps it to disperse properly.

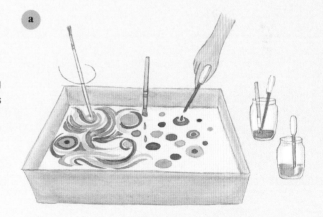

a

2. Lay the card on top of the bath

When you are satisfied with the design, check for air bubbles on the marbling bath surface. If there are any, gently pop them with your fingertips. Take a piece of paper and, holding it at a slight angle to the bath surface, place one end of it onto the surface of the marbling bath,

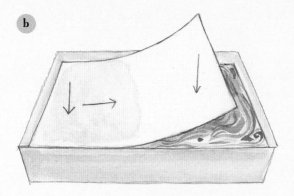
b

then quickly lower the rest of the sheet down onto the surface **(b)**. Be careful not to trap air between the paper and the bath, as this will create a large air bubble, which will prevent some of the paper being printed on. With some paper you can see the shadow of the marbling bath meeting the paper's surface: this will act as a guide as to whether all of the paper is in contact with the bath as you lay the paper down. Try not to let any of the marbling bath flood over the top of the paper as you need this to be clean for the back of the card project.

3. Rinse and dry the marbled card

Lift the paper off of the surface of the marbling bath holding it by its corner and let any excess marbling bath size drip off the paper into the bath. You might experience some bleeding of certain colours; this will rinse off in the water bath leaving marbled colour behind. Place the paper marble-side up in the water bath. Either gently rock the water bath or, holding a corner of the paper, move it in the water to gently to rinse away the excess size. Allow excess water to drip from the paper and then carefully peg the top two corners of the paper on a washing line **(c)**. Allow the paper to dry: when thoroughly dry store the marbled papers together under an even weight to flatten them. If the papers are very cockled, iron the back of them with a warm iron.

c

4. Make the butterfly cards

Next, fold the marbled paper in half – the cards work best when folded landscape but they can be folded and trimmed square. Enlarge the Butterflies templates on the inside front cover of this book to a size that will fit your folded cards, then trace them. Select the best side of marbling of the marbled paper. Make sure the butterfly is the right way up and transfer the traced image centrally onto the bottom half of the inside of the marbled card (see page 10). Carefully cut out the design using a scalpel or craft knife on a cutting mat, making sure that every line is cut through **(d)** and press out the butterfly design. Trim down if needed.

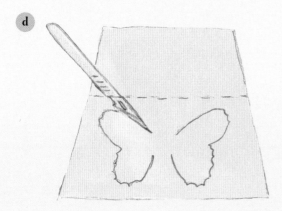
d

PRETTY DECORATIVE PAPERS
combed marbling

This is a project that my children helped me with, producing some lovely decorative papers. These papers can be used for lining cupboards, wrapping gifts or covering notebooks and folders. The great thing about a decorative paper is that each one is an expression of the person who made it – it is unique and beautiful!

YOU WILL NEED

Marbling kit (see page 34), with large trays big enough for your paper

Marbling comb (see page 36)

Large sheets of plain paper – most papers work well it really comes down to trial and error and what you can obtain reasonably. Lining paper cut to the length of gift-wrap and flattened works well as do large, cheap sketchpads of paper

A warm, windless, sunny day!

LEVEL
Easy

METHOD

1. Create the feathered marbling surface

Using your pipettes, drop colour at even intervals on the surface of the marbling bath. Drop other colours one at a time within the first droplets of colour to create concentric circles of colour. Take a marbling comb and place it in one end of the bath, then gently move it down the bath so that it combs through the colours creating a peacock feathered look **(a)**. Lift the comb out.

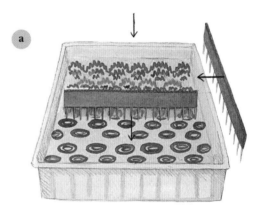

2. Print the paper

Take a large piece of paper, place one end in the bath then lower the rest of the paper quickly and carefully down into the bath (I find laying the paper horizontally easier than laying it vertically). You should be able to see the shadow of the marbling bath meeting the paper's surface: this will act as a guide as to whether all of the paper is in contact with the bath as you lay the paper down. Once the paper is in contact with the bath, lift the paper up by two corners and drain off any excess marbling size. Carefully place it into the water bath, agitate the bath to rinse off the size and any excess pigment. Try not to touch the surface as this can disturb the marbling. Don't leave the paper in the water bath for too long as the paper could get too waterlogged and

fall apart. Drain off any excess water and peg the top corners of the paper on a washing line and leave to dry, if possible in the sun.

3. Variation

For a variation of the technique above, comb the paint droplets vertically and then horizontally to create a finely detailed combed pattern. You can also move the comb from side to side slightly while you are combing through the surface to create a wavy pattern.

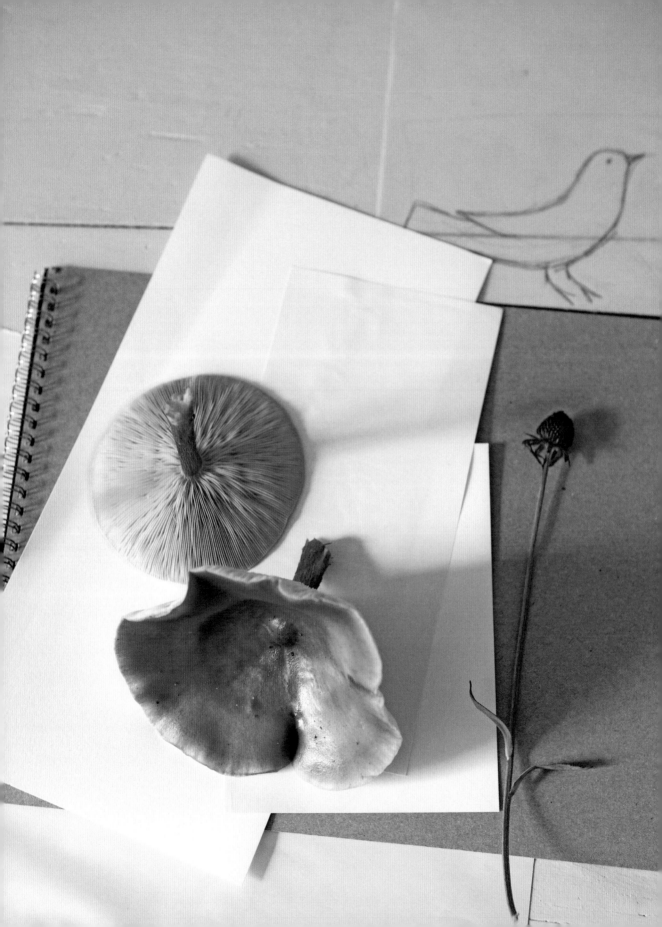

STENCIL-PRINTING

I developed this method of printing while I was running a limited-edition artist book project with students. The project had one condition – everything that appeared in the book had to have been printed by hand.

I had just been on a trip to Russia where I had been inspired by the simplicity and strength of design of the beautiful printed posters and packaging that I had seen. On my return I spent several evenings devising various printing techniques and developed a method of stencil-printing – where a stencilled image was built up using various colour separation stencils, sponge rollers, sponges and stencil brushes – whose results had similar qualities to the posters I had seen. This discovery led me to begin making and selling edition prints of my work.

You can use light-weight card stencils for simple prints, but you will need to create some form of registration for this. The simplest way is to use card and a piece of tracing paper cut to the same dimensions. As long as you line up your tracing paper exactly to the edge of the card when transferring each colour separation for cutting, and you do the same with the paper when you print, there really shouldn't be any problem. This is a good way of trying out the technique cheaply.

If you want something more accurate and durable for long print runs, then low-tack mask film or stencil film is the answer – especially if you want to have detail and more than one colour. It is easier to cut fine details and, because you can see through it, there is more accuracy in printing.

CHILDREN'S BIRTHDAY CARDS
textured stencil-printing on paper

Stencil-printing is a great way of printing in volume. This project takes me back to when I first moved house. I printed 100 moving cards in one day! The cards comprised five colour separations and lettering created using a children's John Bull printing set. Because the colour separations have to be kept quite simple they give the printed image its charm, which is rather lost nowadays with digital printing.

The beauty of stencil-printing is that you can achieve some lovely effects with sponge rollers. The more dense the sponge the more solid the colour, the more open the sponge the softer the colour. You can even use washing-up sponges for stippling and small details.

YOU WILL NEED

Tracing paper

3B pencil

5H pencil

Low-tack mask film or stencil film

Permanent marker pen

Scalpel (X-Acto knife) fitted with 10A blade, or craft knife

Cutting mat

Soft-bodied acrylic paint – crimson, ultramarine blue, lemon yellow, black and white

3 round-headed bristle paintbrushes

Acrylic retarder liquid

A jar of cold water

Old plate or chopping mat, for mixing paints

A6 card blanks, 15 x 11cm (6 x 4¼in) folded size

Scrap paper

Sponge rollers

Stencil brush

LEVEL
Easy

TEMPLATES
Elephant, Duck, Flowers and Train (see page 137), enlarged by 141%

METHOD

1. Cut your stencils

Enlarge each of the templates on page 137 then trace each numbered colour separation, allowing a 1cm (½in) border all the way round each stencil's grey registration border, and transfer the images and their borders onto the paper backing of the low-tack mask or stencil film (see page 10). Trace over the border on the film side of the stencil with a permanent marker pen; this will be used to register the stencil correctly onto the card. Carefully cut

a

out each colour separation using a scalpel or craft knife on a cutting mat. **(a)** For the flower design card you will need to keep the centre circles, as you will need to use them as a mask in the centre of your flower when you come to print it.

2. Mix the paint colours

Add a little acrylic retarder liquid to the mixed colours to prevent the paint from drying out, and a little water if needed, and only mix colours for one card at a time.

I used the following colours:

Elephant card

Stencil 1; grey body – black, white, a little lemon yellow and ultramarine blue

Stencil 2; black details – black with a touch of white to tone it down

Stencil 3; red balloon – crimson, a little lemon yellow and a very small amount of white

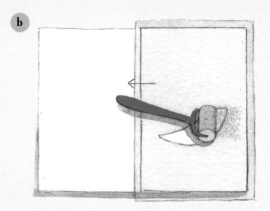

Duck card

Stencils 1 and 2; yellow body – lemon yellow, a little crimson and white

Stencil 3; orange beak, wing and legs – add more crimson to the yellow mix above

Stencil 4; black details – black with a touch of white to tone it down

Stencil 5; blue balloon – ultramarine blue and white with a touch of yellow

Flower card

Stencil 1; green – lemon yellow, white and a little ultramarine blue

Stencil 2; red – crimson

Stencil 3; purple – ultramarine blue, white and a little crimson

Stencil 4; yellow – lemon yellow and a little white

Train card

Stencil 1; red train – crimson, a little lemon yellow and a tiny amount of white to soften the colour

Stencil 2; blue smoke – ultramarine blue, white and a touch of lemon yellow

3. Begin printing the first design

Open out your folded cards. Make sure you print on the right-hand side of the opened card. Using scrap paper try out your sponge roller. With varying pressure and amounts of paint you can create different printed effects. The stencils are numbered, so that they can be printed in order. (It is more efficient to print all of the cards, one colour at a time, letting the cards dry between each colour. If you work methodically in this way, you could print up to 100 cards or more in a single day!) Remove the backing film and position the first stencil for your chosen card design on your card, aligning the permanent marker border with the edge of the card. Roll your sponge roller in the paint so that it is evenly covered. Then roll it over the exposed paper area of the stencil. I usually I do this in one direction, one or two times. **(b)** Gently lift the stencil, (be careful not to rip it, or the paper) and print the rest of your cards. Repeat the process with each colour-separation stencil, lining up the registration border with the edge of the card and the cut stencil with the printed image.

4. Finish printing and add final touches

With small details like the eye detail of the duck, gently stipple your colour with the end of a stencil brush. **(c)**

SUMMER FLOWERS TOTE BAG
stencil-printing on fabric

This little bag reminds me of my grandmother's embroidered tablecloths and her particular passion for anemones. I have printed on two types of bags, ready-made canvas totes and hand-made natural linen bags – I particularly wanted to have a natural linen tote as it looks timeless and works beautifully with the design.

TIP

It is worth printing up a whole bag in all of the colours to make sure that everything is working correctly before printing all of the bags at once. Just make sure that you place each stencil back onto its waxy backing paper after use.

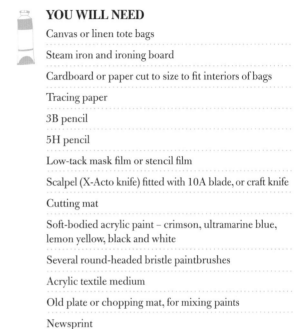

YOU WILL NEED

Canvas or linen tote bags

Steam iron and ironing board

Cardboard or paper cut to size to fit interiors of bags

Tracing paper

3B pencil

5H pencil

Low-tack mask film or stencil film

Scalpel (X-Acto knife) fitted with 10A blade, or craft knife

Cutting mat

Soft-bodied acrylic paint – crimson, ultramarine blue, lemon yellow, black and white

Several round-headed bristle paintbrushes

Acrylic textile medium

Old plate or chopping mat, for mixing paints

Newsprint

7 sponge rollers

Pencil

Tweezers

LEVEL
Intermediate

TEMPLATES
Summer flowers (see page 135), enlarged by 141%

METHOD

1. Prepare the bags
First wash the tote bags to wash out any size in the fabric (see page 11). Allow them to dry and iron them with a hot steam iron. Place a sheet of cardboard or paper – that has been cut to size to fit the interiors of the bags – into each of the bags to prevent any paint seeping through the fabric when you print.

2. Prepare the stencils
Enlarge the template on page 135 then trace each numbered colour separation, allowing a 5cm (2in) border around each stencil's edge to prevent you from accidentally printing on areas other than the design. Transfer the images onto the paper backing of the low-tack mask or stencil film (see page 10). Carefully cut

a

b

c

out each colour separation using a scalpel or craft knife on a cutting mat and remove the waste film. Make sure that you keep the small cut-out flower centres for the anemones to use when printing – in fact, it is worthwhile cutting out two or three extra flower centres as they will lose tack through the print run.

3. Mix the paint colours

I used the following seven paint colours:

Green – lemon yellow, white and a little ultramarine blue
Blue – ultramarine blue, white and a little crimson
Purple – crimson, white and a little ultramarine blue
Red – crimson and a tiny amount of lemon yellow
White – white and a little lemon yellow
Black – black, with a little crimson and ultramarine blue
Yellow – lemon yellow, white and a little crimson

Mix each of the paints with a similar volume of acrylic textile medium. If you like, you could check you are happy with the shades by painting them on a spare piece of material or paper that matches the colour of the totes.

4. Begin printing the design

Cover your work surface with newsprint. Lay your bags on the work surface and, taking stencil 1 (the green foliage stencil), gently peel the stencil film away from the backing paper. Position the stencil 5cm (2in) up from the bottom of the bag, place another sheet of newsprint on top, then

gently smooth the stencil down onto the fabric. Remove the newsprint, load a sponge roller with green paint and roll the paint onto the stencil. **(a)** Roll horizontally first, then repeat with vertical rolls. Apply a little pressure if needed to build up the paint. Gently remove the stencil and repeat this process on all of your bags. Allow the printed image to dry.

5. Continue printing the design

Taking stencil 2 (the red anemone flowers), gently peel the stencil film away from the backing paper. Line the stencil up with the printed green foliage, masking the centres of the flowers with the cut-out flower centres (I use the end of a pencil to press cut-outs into place). Again place a sheet of newsprint on top, then gently smooth the stencil down onto the fabric. Using a clean sponge roller, roll red paint over each flower, being careful not to dislodge the masked centre. **(b)** Gently remove the stencil and repeat this process on all of your bags. Allow the printed images to dry.

6. Finish printing the design

Once printed, remove stencil 2 with tweezers or your fingernails. Continue with each colour separation in turn, using a clean sponge roller for each colour. **(c)** When all the fabric is printed allow it to dry and heat-set the printed fabric with a medium iron (see page 11).

GARDEN BIRDS LAMPSHADE
tonal stencil-printing using dry-brush techniques

This design shows how different tones can be achieved by using varying amounts of pressure with sponge-roller and dry-brush techniques.

This design can be enlarged or reduced to fit shades of different diameters. You may need to measure the overall width and height of each shape to make sure that they will all fit around the shade. For a slightly larger shade, extra space can be allowed between each element to make the design fit.

If you find printing on a lampshade rather daunting, you could print this design onto paper to create a decorative print, using low-tack mask film or stencil film instead of respositional book-covering film.

TIP

Before you begin printing, make sure that your stencil is pressed down firmly; if it is not, paint will seep underneath it, giving your printed design a messy edge. If this does happen, don't despair – allow the paint to dry, cut an extra flower or foliage stencil and use this to mask the accident.

YOU WILL NEED

Metal ruler

Approx. 2.5m (2¾yd) clear repositional book-covering film, or enough to create 12 templates approx. 20 x 25cm (8 x 10in)

Scalpel (X-Acto knife) fitted with 10A blade, or craft knife

Cutting mat

Tracing paper

3B pencil

5H pencil

Cream/white drum-shaped lampshade, approx. 25cm (10in) diameter and 18cm (7in) high, with a fairly smooth surface

Masking tape

Soft-bodied acrylic paint – black

A round-headed bristle paintbrush

Acrylic textile medium

Old plate or chopping mat, for mixing paint

Sponge roller, 5–7.5cm (2–3in) wide

Newsprint

Stencil brush or 2.5cm (1in) flat hog-hair paintbrush

Hairdryer

Scrap paper

LEVEL

Difficult

TEMPLATES

Songthrush, Robin and Wren (see page 133), enlarged by 200% to use on a 25cm (10in) diameter lampshade. The Songthrush template is used once as shown and once more mirrored. The Design layout (see page 133) is a guide to positioning the four separate templates.

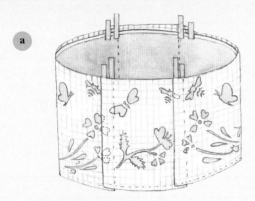

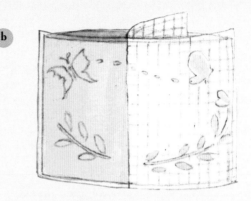

METHOD

1. Prepare the stencils

Enlarge the Songthrush, Robin and Wren templates on page 133, then use the copier to create a mirror image of the Songthrush template. Each template has three colour separations, each for a different tone, so you will need to create three stencils from each template, giving you a total of 12 stencils. Beginning with template 1, the Songthrush, take colour separation template A (red) and measure and cut book-covering film 6mm (¼in) taller than the height of your shade and 5–10cm (2–4in) wider than your template, allowing a border to prevent accidental printing in areas other than the design. Trace the template, centre it on the paper backing of the book-covering film 3cm (1¼in) from the bottom and transfer the design (see page 10). Cut out the stencil using a scalpel or craft knife on a cutting mat. Make sure that you keep the small cut-out circles and details for the butterflies and flowers. On separate, smaller pieces of book-covering film (allowing a generous border) trace, transfer and cut out Songthrush stencil B (blue) and Songthrush stencil C (black). Repeat this process for each of the colour separations of the Songthrush mirror image (template 2), the Robin (template 3) and the Wren (template 4).

2. Prepare the shade

Refer to the Design layout on page 133 for guidance on how to position the four different templates (you will need to use your artistic eye to judge the arrangement). Note that the designs flow into one another, and so you may find that the edges of the stencils overlap slightly; this is

fine, as long as the cut-out shapes don't overlap. Working from the side seam of the shade, use masking tape to position each (paper-backed) stencil A (red) on the shade, and arrange so that all four designs fit around with even spaces between each design. Each design should sit comfortably on the lampshade approximately 2.5cm (1in) from the bottom with approximately 1.5cm (⁵⁄₈in) between each design. (This positioning will ensure a 3mm (¹⁄₈in) overlap of book-covering film either side of the shade's rim to protect it from paint.) Using more masking tape mark the position of where each stencil begins and ends inside the shade **(a)**, writing the template number onto the masking tape to avoid any confusion.

3. Stick down the first stencil

When you are satisfied with where the stencils are positioned, remove all but stencil A of the Songthrush (template 1). Starting at one edge, peel back 2.5cm (1in) of the backing paper. **(b)** Position the stencil and smooth it onto the shade firmly. If the image is crooked, gently lift the stencil off and reposition it, being careful not to let the stencil stick to itself. Once you're happy with the positioning, peel off the rest of the backing paper. Position the small cut-out circles and details for the butterflies and flowers within the stencils.

4. Print the first separation of template 1

Mix the black acrylic paint with a similar volume of acrylic textile medium. Load a sponge roller with the paint and test it on newsprint; it should evenly distribute the paint.

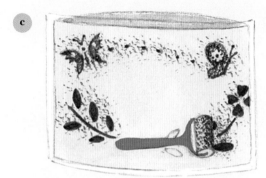

Turn the lampshade onto its side; hold the internal fitting with one hand to keep it steady, and the roller in your other hand. The foliage in my design is has a heavier tone and the butterflies' and bees' wings have a lighter tone. For sections with a heavier tone, apply a little pressure to the roller, rolling over the area several times. **(c)** For sections with a lighter tone, apply less pressure to the roller, rolling over the area just once or twice. If you want the butterflies to be light on the wings and dark on the body, roll over the entire butterfly lightly with a roller and stipple darker areas with a stencil brush. Once you are happy with the printing of this first stencil A, carefully remove the stencil and place it back onto its waxed backing paper. Allow the lampshade to dry (a hairdryer on a warm setting speeds this up).

5. Print the second separation of template 1
Take stencil B (blue) of the Songthrush (template 1) and, using the Design layout on page 133 as a guide, position the stencil, making sure the acorn is about 6mm (¼in) away from the edge of the foliage. Starting at one edge, peel back 2.5cm (1in) of the backing paper. Position the stencil and smooth it onto the shade. Once you're happy with the positioning, peel off the rest of the backing paper and smooth the template into place. Dip a dry stencil brush into the paint and practise some brushstokes on scrap paper, making them as even as possible. Once you are happy, start off by stippling the beak of the songthrush then, working from the head of the bird, follow its shape with long, even strokes, leaving the bird paler in the

middle, then brushing back in from the tail. **(d)** Next, using the sponge roller, lightly roller over the oak leaf and acorn, applying a little pressure at an angle from the bottom edge of the acorn to give it dimension. Remove the stencil and allow the lampshade to dry.

6. Print the third separation of template 1
Take stencil C (black) of the Songthrush (template 1) and, using the Design layout on page 133 as a guide, position the stencil over the thrush and oak leaf. Once you are happy with the position, peel off the backing paper and smooth the surface. Stipple and brush the stencil details with the black paint. Remove the stencil and allow the lampshade to dry.

7. Print the remaining designs
Using the masking tape position markers and the Design layout on page 133 as a guide, repeat steps 3–6 for the remaining three templates (Songthrush mirror image, Robin and Wren), allowing each application of paint to dry before moving onto the next. Remember to print the foliage with heavier tones, the insects with lighter tones, and use the dry brush technique to make the birds darker at their edges and paler in the middle.

FOLK ART BOWLS
stencil-printing on china

This is a satisfying and effective way of creating simple, stylish and individual designs on china. Porcelain paints are very durable, but do keep the painted designs to areas that won't come into contact with cutlery – such as the outsides of bowls and the edges of plates.

The technique takes a little practice, but you can wipe or wash off your design if it is wonky or wrongly spaced, or if there are any smudges or mistakes, as the paint is removable until it is baked. (Have some damp kitchen paper to hand for this purpose, and make sure that you clean up any marks that may have occurred during the printing process before you bake your china.)

It is important to flatten the stencil down well when printing – and even to cut some extra stencils to use if you are decorating a lot of china, in case your stencil loses its stickiness.

YOU WILL NEED

Tracing paper

3B pencil

5H pencil

5 x 7.5cm (2 x 3in) low-tack mask film or stencil film

Scalpel (X-Acto knife) fitted with 10A blade, or craft knife

Cutting mat

Medium oven-proof china bowls

Masking tape

Watercolor pencil

A small make-up sponge

Pebeo Porcelaine 150 paint – scarlet red and abyss black

Damp kitchen paper

Kebab skewer or cocktail stick

LEVEL
Easy

TEMPLATES

Heart, Horse (see inside front cover)

METHOD

1. Prepare the stencils and china
Trace and transfer your chosen template (see page 10) on the inside front cover onto the paper backing of the low-tack mask or stencil film, and carefully cut it out using a scalpel or craft knife on a cutting mat. Remove any sticky labels from the china and wash and dry it thoroughly.

2. Work out the positions of each stencil
Measure the circumference of each bowl by placing a length of masking tape around the outer rim, then gently remove the tape and stick it onto a plastic surface. Use the shape you have cut out of your stencil to work a design so that there is more or less 1cm (½in) between each shape, and mark their positions on the masking tape. **(a)**

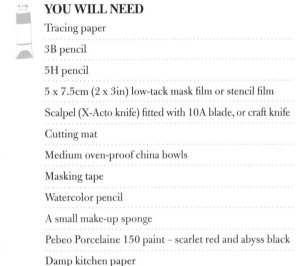

a

3. Mark the stencil positions on the china bowl and begin printing
Reposition the masking tape just below the bowl's outer rim and use a watercolour pencil to mark out the stencil

positions on the bowl's side, positioning the stencil each time so that its top edge is 6mm (¼in) down from the rim of the bowl. Using a small make-up sponge, gently sponge scarlet red or abyss black paint onto the stencil. **(b)** Be careful not to print over its edges. If you have any accidents or misprints wipe them off the bowl with dampened kitchen paper.

4. Finish printing and add details

Carefully remove the stencil and reposition it repeatedly around the side of the bowl, being careful not to smudge the printed shape. If you are printing the horse, once all of the shapes are printed, scratch out the eye detail with the pointed end of a kebab skewer or cocktail stick. **(c)** If it is difficult to scratch out the paint, dampen the tip of

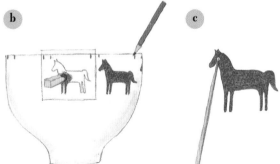

the stick. Allow to dry for 24 hours and then, following the Porcelaine paint instructions, bake your bowls in an oven for 35 minutes at 150°C/300°F/gas mark 2.

RELIEF-PRINTING

The projects in this chapter are all created using relief-printing, which is a very satisfying and immediate printing technique. Each involves either cutting out, carving or engraving, or using things in their natural state. You could even combine a number of techniques to create really exciting prints.

This is where fabric-printing comes into its own. I am still excited by the endless possibilities of design combinations and different printed effects that can be achieved on fabric. It is definitely much more interesting to come up with your own designs for textiles and papers than buying them!

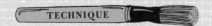

BLOCK-PRINTING

Block-printing is a very effective way of printing onto fabric, papers and cards. It is cheap and easy to do, and designs can range from simple to complicated. Block-printing is traditionally achieved using carved wooden blocks, but another really easy and effective way is to use easy-to-cut craft foam sheets, which can be sourced on the Internet or found in the children's area in craft shops. This technique will give you hours of fun, especially printing numerous design combinations.

BLOCK-MAKING KIT

Tracing paper

3B pencil

5H pencil

2 or 3 sheets of self-adhesive craft foam. If you can't find the self-adhesive version, you can glue the back of it with PVA glue

Scalpel (X-Acto knife) fitted with 10A blade, or craft knife

Cutting mat

Millboard, approx. 2mm (¹/₁₆ in) thick. The card at the back of sketch pads is good for this

Bodkin or metal kebab skewer

Scissors

Sandpaper, for sanding down the rough ends of your wooden blocks

PVA glue and brush

Small wooden blocks – packets are available in some craft shops. Alternatively, cut 5 x 1.5cm (2 x ⁵/₈ in) battening into blocks measuring 5 x 10cm (2 x 4in)

METHOD

1. Trace and transfer the design

Choose a template from the front or back of this book, then trace and transfer the design onto self-adhesive craft foam (see page 10).

2. Cut out the foam

Cut out your design using a scalpel or craft knife on a cutting mat. **(a)** Peel the backing paper off the back of the craft foam and stick your motif onto a piece of millboard.

3. Add details to the motifs

To create dot eye details, pierce and rotate with the end of a bodkin or kebab skewer. For indentation lines and details, draw the bodkin across the foam with some pressure. **(b)**

4. Make the mount

Draw around the craft-foam motif onto its backing millboard, leaving a border roughly 3mm (¹/₈ in) wide. (This mount will prevent the edge of the wooden block from accidentally printing.) Cut this out carefully. (If you find the millboard hard to cut, use scissors to cut off most of it and trim off the excess with a scalpel or craft knife.)

5. Make the block

Sand down the rough ends of your wooden blocks using sandpaper. Using PVA glue, stick the motif centrally onto a 5 x 10cm (2 x 4in) wooden block. **(c)** Allow to dry for a couple of hours and then you are ready to print!

PROJECT...

PATTERNED WRAPPING PAPER & TAGS
block-printing onto paper

Good wrapping paper and tags can be expensive to buy, and so can rubber printing stamps. Here is a way of printing your own paper and tags with home-made foam blocks. The lovely thing about home-made foam blocks is that you can keep them in a shoebox and add new designs to the collection.

TIP

To change the colour on a printing block, wipe the craft foam with a damp cloth a few times and print off onto a scrap piece of paper until clear.

YOU WILL NEED

Block-making kit (see page 58)

Newsprint

Soft-bodied acrylic paint – crimson, cobalt blue, lemon yellow, black and white

3 round-headed bristle paintbrushes

Acrylic retarder liquid

Old plate or chopping mat

Foam roller

For the wrapping paper

A2 sheets of sugar paper, brown paper or lining paper

For the tags

Heavy-weight card

Scissors

Hole punch

Coloured ribbon

LEVEL

Intermediate

TEMPLATES

Boat, Fish, Goose, Shell 1, Shell 2, Shell 3 (see inside back cover)

METHOD

1. Trace designs and make blocks

Trace the template designs of your choice from the inside back cover (see page 10) and follow the instructions for how to make a block on page 58.

2. Prepare to print

Place a few sheets of newsprint onto your work surface. Place the paper that you want to print onto on top of this. Mix black acrylic paint with a little acrylic retarder liquid to prevent the paint from drying out. Make up a cadmium red using crimson, a little lemon yellow and a little retarder. Make a pale blue from

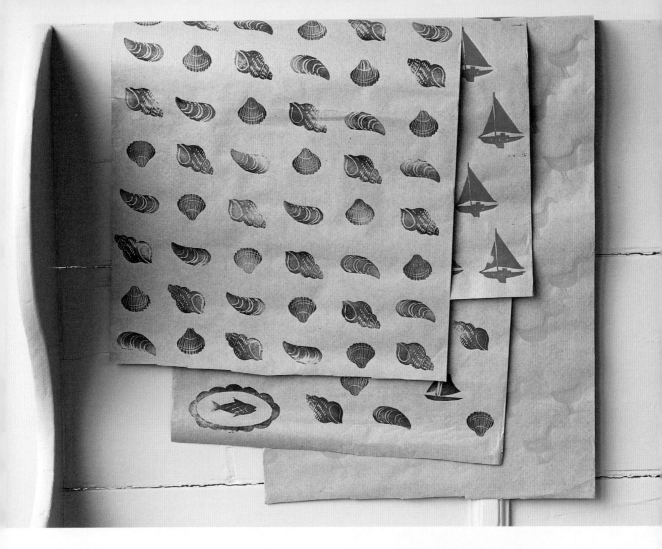

cobalt blue, white, a little lemon yellow and a little retarder. Roll your foam roller in the paint so that it is evenly covered; the paint should sound wispy as you roll it, rather than sticky. Roll over the foam surface of one of your printing blocks with paint. **(a)**

3. Print the paper
With two hands on the block (one for pressure and one for positioning), press down onto your paper and print. **(b)** You can play around with patterns and colour combinations, printing in rows, or alternating different blocks and colours.

Don't worry if the images don't always print properly: the overall effect can be quite pleasing all the same! Allow the printed papers to dry and store either in an under-bed storage box or loosely folded in a large drawer.

4. Print the tags
Print a whole sheet of heavy-weight card and cut out tags from this. Punch with holes and thread with ribbon.

FLYING BIRD CUSHION
block-printing onto fabric

One of my favourite sights is a silhouetted bird against the sky, and this simple block design captures that image. I love the blackbird set against natural or powder-blue linen; you can also include some filigree to produce a more interesting design.

TIP

It is always a good idea to practise printing out designs onto paper before graduating to fabric so that you can work out the spacing between each block, explore pattern possibilities, and make sure that everything is working well.

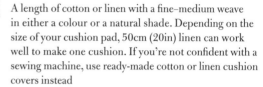

YOU WILL NEED

Block-making kit (see page 58)

A length of cotton or linen with a fine–medium weave in either a colour or a natural shade. Depending on the size of your cushion pad, 50cm (20in) linen can work well to make one cushion. If you're not confident with a sewing machine, use ready-made cotton or linen cushion covers instead

Thick cardboard or paper cut to size to fit inside the cushion covers (if using ready-made cushions)

Newsprint

Masking tape

Metal ruler

Soft-bodied acrylic paint – black

A round-headed bristle paintbrush

Acrylic textile medium

Old plate or chopping mat, for mixing paint

Foam roller

Iron and ironing board

Sewing machine and thread

Shell button fastenings

LEVEL

Intermediate

TEMPLATES

Flying bird (see page 132). Copy this template with or without the filigree details, to suit your preference.

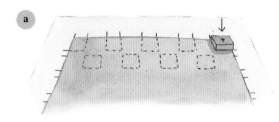

METHOD

1. Trace designs and make blocks
Trace the template design – with or without the filigree – from page 132 and follow the instructions for how to make a block on page 58.

2. Prepare the fabric
Wash the fabric or ready-made cushion covers to remove any size in the fabric (see page 11). Allow to dry and iron with a hot steam iron. If you are using ready-made cushions, place a thick sheet of cardboard or paper – that has been cut to size to fit the interiors of the cushions – inside to prevent any folds from spoiling the printing.

3. Prepare to print
Work in a fairly large, clear space. Cover a table with taped-down newsprint. Mark out the width of your fabric, or cushion covers onto the paper, then mark out where you want to print your printing block. I find that the best way to do this is to mark out the block at both ends of the fabric and the middle and then work out how many motifs can be printed equally in between. For the second row mark out a distance of about 1cm (½in) down from the bottom of the first row of blocks at the side of your paper as a rough guide, as the second row will be printed as a staggered repeat. Using a ruler, roughly mark a line at the side of the paper where the baseline of each row will be. To ensure that you print with the block the right way up, draw an arrow on the back of the block. **(a)**

4. Begin printing
Squeeze out black acrylic paint onto a plate or mat, then add a similar volume of acrylic textile medium to the paint. Roll your foam roller in the paint so that it is evenly covered. Roll over the foam surface of your printing block with paint. **(b)** Make sure the block is the right way up, then print the first row of motifs, pressing the block firmly onto the fabric and reapplying paint between each printing. Don't worry if the block doesn't always print uniformly; this effect can add to the fabric's hand-made quality.

5. Finish printing
To print the next row of motifs, position the block 1cm (½in) down from the bottom of the first row of blocks, in between two birds, to create a staggered repeat. If you find that your fabric is longer than your table, start to move it off the edge of the table away from you as you print. Just ensure that it doesn't fall onto itself by draping it over a chair or two. If you are printing on a ready-made cushion, allow the printed side to dry before turning the cushion cover over to repeat the process on the other side. Once your material is printed, allow it to dry and heat-set the paint with a medium iron (see page 11). Print off any excess paint on the blocks and allow them to dry before storing them.

6. Sew your cushion
If you have printed lengths of fabric, use a sewing machine to make it up into a simple envelope cushion with shell button fastenings.

COUNTRY HOUSE TABLE LINEN
two-colour block-printing

This project shows you how to make larger blocks and create two-colour printed designs.

The design I've used is inspired by animals and the countryside, and works beautifully with natural linen. I made the napkins by folding and cutting the pre-washed linen (see page 11) into 40 x 40cm (16 x 16in) squares, and the placemats by cutting the linen into 48 x 63cm (19 x 25in) rectangles. I folded and ironed the top and bottom edges twice to make a 1cm (½in) hem, securing the bottom and top corners with a flower pin. I hemmed them and removed the pin while sewing, and then sewed the two side hems.

TIP

To distinguish the napkins from the placemats, and to make the set a little more interesting, I have used a different design for each. For the napkins, I have printed the four corners with leaves and acorns. For the placemats, I have printed the four corners with leaves and acorns and the four sides with the country house.

YOU WILL NEED

Block-making kit (see page 58), but with larger pieces of wood for the blocks as follows:

    2 blocks 5 x 18cm (2 x 7in) for templates 1 and 2

    1 block 5 x 10cm (2 x 4in) for template 3

    1 block 5 x 5cm (2 x 2in) for template 4

Prepared linen placemats and napkins (see page 11)

Iron and ironing board

Newsprint

Soft-bodied acrylic paint – cobalt blue, lemon yellow, black and white

2 round-headed bristle paintbrushes

Acrylic textile medium

Old plate or chopping mat, for mixing paint

Scrap fabric

Marker pens in a variety of colours

Foam roller

LEVEL

Intermediate

TEMPLATES

Country house, Spaced leaves, Corner leaves, Acorn (see inside front cover)

METHOD

1. Trace designs and begin to make blocks

Trace the template designs from the inside back cover and follow instructions for how to make a block on page 58, but transfer the scenes onto the millboard as well as to the craft foam; this will act as a guide to positioning the craft foam pieces on the millboard to make up the designs. Next transfer the dotted edge of each template design centrally onto its appropriate block of wood by lining up the template borders with the edge of the wood; this will act as a guide for positioning the millboard. Use a thicker pencil to go over the dotted lines on the tracing paper so that it will transfer to the wooden surface. Cut out all the separate elements of the designs from the craft foam and stick the pieces into place on the millboard. **(a)**

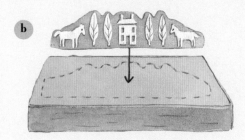

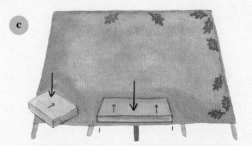

2. Add details to the motifs

To create dot eye details, pierce and rotate with the end of a bodkin or kebab skewer. For indentation lines and details, draw the bodkin across the foam with some pressure. Draw around the designs on the millboard, leaving a 3mm (1/8 in) border. For the Country house, cut out the whole design on the millboard and stick it onto the appropriate piece of wood with PVA glue, lining the design up with the dotted edge of the template on the wooden block. **(b)** For the Spaced leaves, Corner leaves and Acorn, cut out the motifs individually from the millboard and stick them into place on their appropriate pieces of wood with PVA glue. Allow the wooden blocks to dry.

3. Prepare to print

Iron the prepared napkins and placemats. Prepare your workspace by placing newsprint onto a flat work surface. Mix black acrylic paint with a similar volume of textile medium. Make up a green paint using cobalt blue, lemon yellow and a little white and mix this with a similar volume of textile medium. It is a good idea to test-print your blocks on a piece of scrap fabric to make sure that everything is printing correctly. Make sure that the millboard isn't printing; if it is, trim it off carefully with a scalpel or craft knife.

4. Print the oak leaves

Lay the placemat on the covered work surface and mark out onto the newsprint the width, height and centre line of the placemat in different colours of marker pen along a baseline. Line up the Spaced leaves block so that the image will print 2cm (3/4in) in from one edge of the placemat, centrally. **(c)** With pencil, mark the edges of the block onto the newsprint as a guide to the registration of the second block. Roll the foam roller in the green paint:

the roller should not be over-laden with paint as this can fill in the details. Roll over the design and print the block, avoiding printing on the hem edge. Apply pressure with the palm of your hand but don't rock the block. Turn the placemat around and print the other three sides in the same way, rolling up with paint before each print. Repeat for the other placemats and allow to dry.

5. Print the corner leaves

Take the Corner leaves block, and position it in one corner of the placemat, so that the edges of the leaves are about 2cm (3/4in) in from the edge of the placemat. Again mark the edges of the block in pencil and the corner of the placemat in coloured marker pen on the newsprint as a guide for the rest of the printing – this will also be the same for the napkins. Roll over the design in green paint and print all four corners of all the placemats and napkins with the oak leaf design, rolling up with paint before each print. Allow the printed leaves to dry.

6. Print the house scene

Place the Country house block within the drawn guides, so that it will print in the same place as the Spaced leaves block. Roll the block with black paint and print the design, making sure that you apply even pressure over the block. Repeat on all sides of all the placemats and allow to dry.

7. Print the acorn

Line up the Acorn block so that it will print in the centre of the corner leaves, roll over the design in black paint and print. Repeat for each corner of each placemat and napkin. Allow the placemats and napkins to dry and heat-set the printed images with a medium iron (see page 11).

USING A LINO-CUTTING TOOL

Lino-cutters are notorious for causing gouge accidents, particularly if you are working with a hard lino surface. As long as you are gentle and careful using these tools you should not encounter any problems because the surface you are cutting into for the projects in this book is relatively soft. Nevertheless, it is advisable to try to keep your fingers clear when you are cutting.

LINO-CUTTING KIT

A lino-cutting tools set, which includes:

– a blade remover
– 5 assorted wooden-handled cutters: V, U 2mm, U 3mm, U 4mm and a cutting knife

TIP

Always cut away from yourself – never in the direction of your body and hands – and always keep your 'holding' hand positioned behind your 'carving' hand, turning the material you are cutting around as you work. Keep your face a good distance from your work while you are cutting.

The U cutter

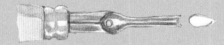

The V cutter

The U cutter will give a wider cut, whereas the V cutter will give a finer cut.

METHOD

1. Cutting with a lino-cutter

Holding your lino-cutter firmly in your dominant hand, with your other hand positioned behind your carving hand, pierce the surface of the material you are cutting at an angle **(a)**, decrease the angle between the cutter and the material while cutting **(b)** and exit with an upwards move **(c)**. Cutting in this manner means that the cut will be wide upon entrance and narrower upon exit, especially if the angles are exaggerated.

2. Vary your cutting angle for effect

The more upright you hold the cutter when cutting, the deeper the cut. The more shallow the angle between the cutter and the material when cutting, the finer the cut. If you exit abruptly you will give your cut a squarer end. Often these characteristics are worked into lino-cut designs.

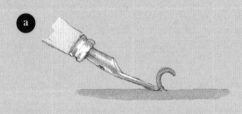

DRAGONFLY & BUTTERFLY DRAWER PAPERS
potato-printing onto paper

Until recently I had always regarded potato-printing as a rather messy, crude form of printing, and something you did only in primary school. Well, I was wrong! If you use lino-cutting tools you can create beautiful prints using potatoes. They are a perfect printing material because they are easy to carve and cut, and they have a little "give" in them.

I love the gold paint used against the pastel colours in this project. Although it is a less delicate design, the blue butterfly paper reminds me of the gold papers lavishing the walls of Pushkin's Palace in Russia.

YOU WILL NEED

Large potatoes

Smooth blade knife

Chopping board

Kitchen paper

3B pencil

White copier paper

Scissors

Charcoal or watercolour pencil – a Stabilo Woody 3 in 1 pencil works particularly well

Craft knife

Lino-cutter No. 1 V (small)

Bodkin or kebab skewer

Soft-bodied acrylic paint – gold

A round-headed bristle paintbrush

Old plate or chopping mat, for mixing paint

Sponge roller

A2-sized sugar paper – pale blue, green and dusky pink work particularly well with the gold

LEVEL

Easy

TEMPLATES

Butterfly and Dragonfly x 3 (see inside front cover)

TIP

If you do a lot of potato-printing you may notice that your cutters begin to rust. Make sure that you clean them carefully and allow them to dry in a warm environment after use.

METHOD

1. Prepare the potatoes

Cut your potatoes in half with a smooth blade knife on a chopping board. **(a)** Place the cut halves onto a sheet of kitchen paper to absorb some of the wetness.

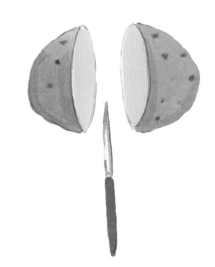

a

2. Prepare the templates

Draw around the cut potato halves onto copier paper **(b)**; this might make the paper a little damp, so allow it to dry before continuing. Cut out the paper shapes with scissors and lay them centrally over the Butterfly 1, Butterfly 2 and Dragonfly templates on the inside front cover. Trace over the templates with a charcoal or watercolour pencil, making sure that you draw with a firm, bold line.

3. Transfer the design

Line up each cut potato with its paper template, then press the potato down onto the right side of the template drawing. The potato should still have a little dampness to it (if not, you can wet it with some damp kitchen paper) which will make the paper template stick to the potato. Lift the potato up: the paper should be attached to the cut surface. Smooth over the back of the template with your fingers. This should transfer the charcoal or watercolour pencil onto the potato. Remove the paper and try not to smudge the drawing. **(c)**

b

4. Cut around the design outline

Using a craft knife and taking care not to cut yourself, gently and slowly cut around the butterfly or dragonfly design, turning your potato as you cut. Try to cut down about 3–6mm (⅛–¼in) into the potato. When you have cut around the whole design, turn the potato onto its side. At about 3–6mm (⅛–¼in) from the edge of the potato, gently carve in from the side towards the cut edges of the butterfly and pull away the potato that's not part of the design. **(d)** Be very careful as you do this, as part of the design could come away by mistake.

c

5. Carve out the details

Once you have cut around the butterfly, tidy up your design with the edge of your knife. Then, using a No. 1 V lino-cutter (see page 68), gently carve out the details of the butterfly or dragonfly, digging a little deeper to differentiate between its wings and its body. **(e)** To create dot eye details, pierce and rotate with the end of a bodkin or kebab skewer. Once the potato designs are cut, place the designs face-down onto kitchen paper and allow them to dry, ideally for 24 hours.

6. Shape a "handle"

You might find it helpful to cut a wedge from either side of the rounded back of the potato (leaving a large block "handle" in the middle) to make it easier to hold and print with. **(f)** Just be careful not to cut away any of the design!

7. Prepare your printing area

Work on a clear, level work surface – a kitchen table covered in newspaper or a wipeable tablecloth would work well. Squeeze out some gold acrylic paint onto a plate or mat; make sure that it isn't too thick as this can fill in the design details. Roll the sponge roller in the paint so that it is evenly covered.

8. Print the papers

When you are ready to print, roll paint onto the butterfly or dragonfly design on the potato and press the potato firmly down onto a sheet of coloured sugar paper. Repeat the process as desired over the paper, rolling up with more paint before each print. If the design begins to fill in too much, wash the potato to remove excess paint, then dry it with kitchen paper and continue. You can play around with patterns and colour combinations, printing in rows, or alternating different designs and colours. I have printed a staggered repeat and a variation by printing the butterflies and dragonflies at angles to each other. Allow the printed papers to dry and store either in an under-bed storage box or loosely folded in a large drawer.

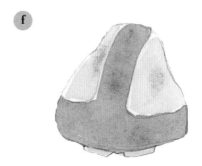

PROJECT...

AUTUMN TABLECLOTH
potato-printing onto fabric

This project focuses on carving positive and
negative spaces in potatoes using lino-cutting
tools. I have used cotton drill for my tablecloth
as it has a tactile quality, is good to print on
and is very reasonable to buy. Alternatively, you
could print on a ready-made white tablecloth.
This is a very good project for practising lino-
cutting techniques and, if you are unhappy with
a design, you can simply slice off the surface
and start again!

YOU WILL NEED

Large potato

Smooth blade knife

Chopping board

Kitchen paper

3B pencil

White copier paper

Scissors

Charcoal or watercolour pencil, such as Stabilo Woody 3 in 1

Lino-cutters No. 1 V (small) and No. 2 U (small)

Kebab skewer

Soft-bodied acrylic paint – crimson, ultramarine blue,
lemon yellow and white

2 round-headed bristle paintbrushes

Acrylic textile medium

Old plate or chopping mat, for mixing paint

2 sponge rollers

Cotton drill fabric, 150cm (60in) square, prepared for
printing (see page 11)

Sewing machine and thread

LEVEL
Easy

TEMPLATES
Pear 1, Pear 2 (see page 132), enlarged to fit your potato

METHOD

1. Prepare the potatoes

Cut your potato in half with a smooth blade knife on a
chopping board. Place the cut halves onto a sheet of
kitchen paper to absorb some of the wetness. Enlarge
the two Pear templates on page 132 and transfer
them as described in steps 2 and 3 of the Dragonfly
& Butterfly Drawer Papers (see page 70).

a

b

c

2. Prepare the negative space pear design

Take the Pear 1 potato half and, using a No. 1 V lino-cutter (see page 68), gently carve out all the lines of the design, turning the potato as you cut around the curves and shaking off any wet potato cuttings. Ideally, for this project, your carve lines should be 1–2mm (¹⁄₁₆in or less) deep. For the filigree details, as soon as you have entered at an angle, exit to keep the cut small. **(a)** Pierce with the point of a kebab skewer to create the dot details for the pear's skin. Place the cut design face-down onto kitchen paper and allow it to dry, ideally for 24 hours.

3. Prepare the positive space pear design

Take the Pear 2 potato half and, using the No. 1 V lino-cutter, gently carve around the positive design, taking care when cutting around the pear's stalk and leaf. Make sure you leave a 1–2mm (¹⁄₁₆in or less) gap between the edge of the filigree details and the border of the design. With a No. 2 U cutter, cut away areas that are not part of the design. **(b)** Use the No. 1 V cutter for any cuts around fine details. Again allow the cut potato to dry for 24 hours.

4. Prepare your printing area

For this project I used my kitchen table covered in an old plastic tablecloth and had my paints on another protected surface. It is important that your surface is flat as this can affect the printed results. If your table is like mine with a few time-worn grooves in it, place an old blanket under the plastic cloth to even it out.

5. Mix the paint

Mix lemon yellow, white and a little ultramarine blue with a similar volume of acrylic textile medium to make a green

colour. Mix crimson, white and a little lemon yellow with a similar volume of textile medium to make a peachy pink colour. Roll a sponge roller into each colour and roll out each onto a clean part of the mixing plate. Make sure that the paint isn't too thick as this can fill in the design details; the paint should sound wispy as you roll it, rather than sticky.

6. Prepare to print

For this project it is better to print alternating colours rather than one colour at a time to avoid muddling and mistakes. Because the design takes a little time to print, it is important to remain focused, as it is easy to print the wrong colour, or print the potato the wrong way up! (It may be worthwhile marking an arrow with a marker pen on the back of each potato half to indicate the right way up of the design, and even indicating the colour you are using.)

7. Print the cloth

When you are ready to print, roll peachy pink paint onto the surface of the Pear 1 potato half. Press the potato firmly down onto the prepared fabric at one end, 2.5cm (1in) down from the top edge and corner. Roll green paint onto the surface of the Pear 2 potato half and print 1cm (½in) apart from the Pear 1 design. Try to keep to a line as you print, as it is easy to go off at an angle. **(c)** Follow the top edge and sides of the table for a useful guide. If you find that your fabric is longer than your table, start to move it off the edge of the table away from you as you print. Just ensure that it doesn't fall onto itself by draping it over a chair or two. This design is an alternating colour repeat. Once you have completed the design allow it to dry for a few hours and then heat-set the fabric with a medium iron (see page 11) and hem the fabric's edges.

BOTANICAL CURTAIN
two-colour relief-printing with found things

Nature creates the most beautiful foliage and flowers, and their likeness can be very difficult to reproduce by hand. I have found that printing with "found" things can be the most satisfying way of printing, and it works wonderfully well with many plants – it really does capture their natural beauty. All of the detail is there, so most of the hard work is done for you leaving you to enjoy printing in different colourways and colour combinations. It is so easy that it is something that children could do!

The fabric I have used for the curtain here is a light-weight muslin, which is a lovely natural material to work with. It takes the printing process well and the end result is a very effective net curtain – I am sure I will never buy a lace net curtain again!

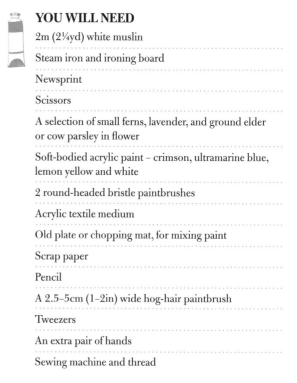

YOU WILL NEED

2m (2¼yd) white muslin

Steam iron and ironing board

Newsprint

Scissors

A selection of small ferns, lavender, and ground elder or cow parsley in flower

Soft-bodied acrylic paint – crimson, ultramarine blue, lemon yellow and white

2 round-headed bristle paintbrushes

Acrylic textile medium

Old plate or chopping mat, for mixing paint

Scrap paper

Pencil

A 2.5–5cm (1–2in) wide hog-hair paintbrush

Tweezers

An extra pair of hands

Sewing machine and thread

LEVEL
Easy

a   b   c

METHOD

1. Prepare the work area and fabric

Wash the muslin to wash out any size in the fabric (see page 11). Allow to dry and iron with a hot steam iron. Cover your work surface with newsprint; make sure that the floor is clean, as the fabric will drop to the floor as it is printed. Lay the prepared fabric out on the work surface. Cut up several pieces of newsprint so they are a little larger than the flowers and foliage.

2. Mix the paint

Mix the following paint colours. (Try to match the colours of the foliage by adding a little colour at a time.)

Minty green – ultramarine blue, lemon yellow and white
Lavender – crimson, ultramarine blue and a little white

Mix each of the paints with a similar volume of acrylic textile medium. It is a good a idea to test print your foliage on scrap paper first to work out a rough pattern repeat and to make sure that the plants print well. My design is a half-drop staggered repeat design.

3. Plot out the design

Mark spacing marks in pencil onto the newsprint above the top edge of the muslin to achieve an evenly spaced design; I usually mark out the middle, both ends and then equally in-between. Plot out the first row of your design; you may choose to print just one fern or flower here, or to alternate between a couple of different items. Then mark out the next row half a drop down as an initial guide for the design.

4. Print the first plant onto the muslin

Apply minty green paint to the first plant with a hog-hair paintbrush **(a)** and carefully lay it down onto the muslin, trying not to let your fingers touch the fabric. Place a small piece of newsprint over the plant, smooth over the paper with the palm of your hand, applying an even pressure, then lift off the newsprint and plant with clean fingers or tweezers – you should have a printed impression of the plant on the fabric. **(b)** Apply more paint to the plant: if you want the plant to face the other way apply paint to its other side and place it upon the muslin and repeat the process. As you can see in the design I varied different plant heads and ferns and printing in between them in a half-staggered design.

5. Continue printing, moving the fabric

If you find that your fabric is longer than your table, move it off the edge of the table away from you as you print, ensuring that it doesn't fall onto itself by draping it over a chair or two. Each time you move the printed fabric you will need assistance in lifting it so that you can refresh the newsprint underneath – this is to avoid any seepage of paint from the printing to the clean unprinted fabric. When printing the lavender, paint lavender paint on the flowers and minty green paint on the stem. **(c)** When all the fabric is printed allow it to dry and heat-set the printed fabric with a medium iron (see page 11), then hem the top edge.

FEATHER TABLE RUNNER
one-colour relief-printing with found things

There are so many different kinds of feathers floating around in my garden that I can't resist collecting them. This printing method is a way of capturing their beauty.

The lovely thing about this project is that you don't need any drawing or painting skills to create beautiful fabric, just the ability to print the feathers in an evenly spaced pattern or staggered rows. There are lots of possibilities for varying the printing. You could print the feathers in a different coloured paint or onto a different coloured background to make cushions, tablecloths or even curtains that complement the design scheme in your home.

Most fine-weave natural fabrics work very well with this printing technique and, although it takes a little time to complete, the effects are quite amazing.

YOU WILL NEED

Grey-blue linen – I used a 50cm (20in) length that was 150cm (60in) wide. Make sure that you have enough to make a table runner for your table

Steam iron and ironing board

Newsprint

Scissors

Selection of around 20 similar-sized feathers – you can buy clean feathers from craft shops if you need to

Pencil

Off-cut of fabric or sheet of scrap paper

Soft-bodied acrylic paint – ultramarine blue, black and white

A round-headed bristle paintbrush

Chair

Acrylic textile medium

Old plate or chopping mat, for mixing paint

Sponge roller

Tweezers

An extra pair of hands

Grey-blue thread for finishing the runner

LEVEL
Easy

METHOD

1. Prepare the work area and fabric

Wash the linen to wash out any size in the fabric
(see page 11). Allow to dry and iron with a hot steam
iron. Cover your work surface with newsprint; make sure
that the floor is clean, as the fabric may drop to the floor
as it is printed. Cut up 50 squares of newsprint that are
larger than your feathers. There are two ways of printing
your fabric: if your table is big enough, lay the whole
length of fabric right-side up on the table; if you have less
space, lay the fabric vertically in front of you (this does
mean that the fabric has to be moved over the table and
the paper underneath has to be refreshed as you print,
but you may find it easier to focus on the design this way).

2. Plot out the design

As an initial guide for the design, arrange feathers at
opposite angles evenly spaced along the top edge of the
fabric and mark little arrows in pencil on the newsprint
above. I have tried to create a falling feather design,
staggering the feathers by printing them at angles and the
opposite way up from each other so that the design feels
quite natural. Practise printing with a few spare feathers
onto an off-cut of fabric or sheet of scrap paper to get the
hang of printing with them and to work out the design.

3. Mix the paint and roll up the first feather

Mix ultramarine blue, black and a little white with a similar
volume of acrylic textile medium to make a soft black
(a pure black would be too hard). Roll the sponge roller

into the paint, rolling the roller several times onto flat part
of the plate or chopping mat so that it is not too sticky
as this would fill in some of the definition of the feathers.
Gently roll paint onto the front of the feather. **(a)**

4. Print the first feather

Lay the feather face down onto the fabric, place a piece
of newsprint on top of it and smooth over the paper with
the palm of your hand, applying an even pressure. **(b)**
Lift off the newsprint and feather with clean fingers or
a pair of tweezers.

5. Finish printing

You will find as you print that the feathers will begin to fill
in and you will have to fan out parts of the feather with
your fingers to maintain a natural shape. This will involve
washing your hands often to keep the fabric clean. Try
to use different feathers throughout the design; this will
also allow the over-used feathers to dry out so that they
can be used again. Progress down the fabric, keeping the
feathers evenly spaced so that the overall design works
well. When all the fabric is printed allow it to dry and heat-
set the printed fabric with a medium iron (see page 11),
then hem the edges of the fabric.

LETTERHEADS, ENVELOPES & TAGS
relief-printing with home-made rubber stamps

This project is a great way of acquainting yourself with lino-cutting techniques and creating personalized rubber stamps. Its success depends on the kind of pencil erasers you use – it's not impossible to find large erasers that cut easily, but it can be a challenge. It is worth buying a variety to see which make are the best to carve, and at least they have two to four surfaces that can be cut. This technique, though cheap, is not as effective or easy as that using Speedy-Carve (see page 82), so it is best to keep to simpler, less detailed designs.

YOU WILL NEED
Tracing paper

3B pencil

5H pencil

Lino-cutters No. 1 V (small) and No. 2 U (small)

A variety of pencil erasers – the larger the better!

Plain writing paper, envelopes and tags

Black archival inkpad

Kitchen paper

LEVEL
Easy

TEMPLATES
Rubber stamp x 6 (see back inside cover)

METHOD

1. Trace and transfer the design
Depending on the size of your erasers you may have to reduce or enlarge the template designs. Trace and transfer your choice of the Rubber stamp templates onto the surface of your erasers (see page 10). Because we are tracing and transferring the template design, the design will print the right way round. However, it is important to remember (especially with regard to numbers and letters) that if you create your own design and draw it directly onto the surface of an eraser, the image will print back to front. So unless you have traced and transferred your design so that it prints the right way round you should draw and cut it out back to front.

2. Carve out the design
Using a No. 1 V lino-cutter and a No. 2 U lino-cutter (see page 68), gently carve out the details of each of the template designs onto the erasers. The template designs are negative space "white on black" designs, so everything

you cut out will remain white. Keep your fingers clear of the lino cutters. If you cut gently, holding the lower part of the eraser and turning it as you cut, there should be no danger of gouging yourself. If there is too much resistance the eraser may not be suitable for this task and will have to be popped into a pencil case instead. Cut out the vertical lines first **(a)**, then the horizontals.

3. Print the design

Once you have carved your erasers you are ready to
print the designs onto your writing paper and envelopes.
Press the eraser into the ink pad being careful not to
catch the plastic edges of the ink pad on the eraser as
this can permanently damage the printing surface. Check
that the eraser is evenly covered with ink, then hold the
eraser over the writing paper to position it, making sure it
is centred, with a small border along the top edge. Press
down all areas of the eraser firmly onto the writing paper
being careful not to move it. Carefully lift the eraser up
and away – you should have a lovely print. Continue
to print several sheets and experiment with the border
designs and where you position the image. Once you have
finished printing, rinse the erasers under a warm tap and
dry them with kitchen paper.

TEATIME GREETINGS CARD
one-colour lino-cut printing

My memories of using lino at art college are not happy ones. The lino was so hard I would make mistakes when cutting and have very sore hands at the end of it – it was a printmaking process I didn't explore further. (Incidentally, if you do use lino, a good tip is to warm it in the oven to soften it before carving.)

But Speedy-Carve has changed this! Because it is soft it is like cutting into firm butter, which lessens the chances of making mistakes and hurting your hands with the cutters. And because it has a little "give" in it, you can print without the use of a relief press. The only downside is that it is more expensive than ordinary lino. As a result, it is best used for cards, small prints and rubber stamps.

TIP

You can either buy tubes or pots of water-soluble printing ink, or a pot of block-printing medium that can be added to acrylic paint. Throughout the book I have used soft-bodied acrylic. It is recommended to use firm-bodied acrylic with the block-printing medium. However, I have used soft-bodied acrylic with block-printing medium for the projects in this book and it has worked very well.

YOU WILL NEED

Tracing paper

3B pencil

5H pencil

7.5 x 10cm (3 x 4in) piece of Speedball Speedy-Carve block

Lino-cutters No. 1 V (small) and No. 2 U (small)

Scalpel (X-Acto knife) fitted with 10A blade, or craft knife

Soft-bodied acrylic paint – crimson, cobalt blue and white

A round-headed bristle paintbrush

Block-printing medium

Old plate or chopping mat, for mixing paint

Foam roller

Newspaper

Newsprint

A6 card blanks, 15 x 11cm (6 x 4¼in) folded size to fit in C6 envelopes

Brayer (optional)

C6 envelopes

LEVEL

Intermediate

TEMPLATES

Teapot (see page 132), enlarged by 141%

METHOD

1. Trace and transfer the design

Enlarge the Teapot template on page 132, then trace and transfer it (see page 10) so that the image is centered on the Speedy-Carve block. Go over any faint lines with pencil. The image should appear back to front on the block so that when it is printed it will print the correct way round.

2. Carve the design with the V cutter

Using a No. 1 V lino-cutter (see page 68), gently carve out the detail of the template design on the block, turning the block when carving around curves and following the drawn lines of the design. To create small dot details, press the cutting tool into the block at a right angle, turn the block around 180 degrees and remove the lino-cutter. To create finer dot details, use a scalpel or craft knife to cut a small circle and lever underneath to ease it out. It is always best to carve away from a design to avoid cutting into it but, for the spout tip, if you carve towards the spout centre and flick up the cutter, the cuts should meet at a fine point to form the "V" of the spout, as the cutter carves wider on entrance and narrower on exit. (Practise this before you do it for real!)

a   b   c

3. Carve the background out with the U cutter

Once you have carved out your design, brush away any loose carvings. At this point it is worth making a few proof prints with your block (which will give you a "white on black" negative image), as this will give you a good idea of how the final image will be printed, highlighting any additional cuts you may need to make. Wash and dry the block. Using a No. 2 U lino-cutter and being careful not to cut into the positive design, cut away those areas that are not part of the design. **(a)** Use the No. 1 V lino-cutter for any cuts around fine details. Once you've finished cutting your image, use a scalpel or craft knife to cut away the Speedy-Carve block to leave an oval-shaped design. Brush off any loose carvings.

4. Prepare the block-printing ink

Mix crimson and cobalt blue paint with a little white to make a lavender blue, then add block-printing medium at a ratio of 2:3. Mix thoroughly with a hog-hair paintbrush and leave for a few minutes to get tacky (this is especially important if you are using soft-bodied acrylic paint).

5. Prepare the printing area

Traditionally a brayer is used to apply ink to the block when lino-cut printing. However, I have found that a foam roller is best with this ink as it gives a good, even coverage to the block. Place a few sheets of newspaper onto a flat work surface next to the rolled-out ink; this will be the inking-up station. Place a piece of newsprint onto a flat area where you are going to print, along with your blank card, so that the two areas are separate from each other. As this is a landscape card design, you should open out the card and position the block over the bottom half of the card, making sure that it will print centrally.

6. Ink up the block

Using the foam roller, roll up a little ink onto the old plate or chopping mat. The ink should sound wispy as you roll it, rather than sticky. Lightly roll the ink over the image so that it is evenly covered. **(b)** If you are too liberal with the ink you might find that the block shifts as you print it and some of the details may fill in.

7. Print the design

There are two ways of printing the block: either place the block ink-side down on the card and, without shifting it, place the palm of your hand on top. Carefully apply pressure, lifting and repositioning your palm to make sure that all areas of the block have received the same amount of pressure **(c)**; alternatively you can carefully roll a brayer over the back of the block, applying a little pressure as you roll – this seems to lessen the chances of the block shifting and applies an even pressure over the whole of the block. If you find that other cut-out areas of the block are still printing, carve these away some more and brush off the block. Once you have finished printing your cards allow them to dry. Once the cards have dried, write your message in them and place into C6 envelopes ready to send. Gently wash the block and dry it with kitchen paper so it can be used again.

LITTLE BOAT PICTURE
two-colour lino-cut printing

This little boat picture is inspired by holidays in Dorset and Devon, on the south coast of England. It is a simple design but it is effective because of its two printed colours. The picture makes a lovely gift, especially when presented in a wooden frame.

This process takes a little planning: it involves creating templates for two colours that are the same size as the plate, and two stages of cutting and printing the plate. The first cuts are for the details and accents on the background colour that will show the cream of the paper; the second cuts are the overall image.

YOU WILL NEED

Tracing paper

3B pencil

5H pencil

7.5 x 10cm (3 x 4in) piece of Speedball Speedy-Carve block

Lino-cutters No. 1 V (small) and No. 2 U (small)

Newspaper

Newsprint

Medium-weight cream paper cut to size – approx. four times the size of the print

Soft-bodied acrylic paint – cobalt blue, lemon yellow, black and white

A round-headed bristle paintbrush

Block-printing medium

Old plate or chopping mat, for mixing paint

Foam roller

Brayer (optional)

Craft knife

LEVEL

Intermediate

TEMPLATES

Little boat 1 and Little boat 2 (see page 138)

METHOD

1. Trace and transfer template 1

Trace and transfer (see page 10) the Little boat 1 template on page 138 onto a piece of Speedy-Carve so that the template borders are lined up with the edges of the block. **(a)** Go over any faint lines with pencil. The image should appear back to front on the block so that when it is printed it will print the correct way round.

2. Carve the design with the V cutter

Using a No. 1 V lino-cutter (see page 68), gently carve out the detail of the template design on the block, turning the block when carving around curves and following the drawn lines of the design. Once you have carved out your design, brush away any loose carvings.

3. Prepare the printing area

Place a few sheets of newspaper onto flat work surface next to where your ink will be rolled out; this will be the inking-up station. Place a piece of newsprint and printing paper onto a flat clean area where you are going to print, so that the two areas are separate from each other.

4. Prepare the block-printing ink

Mix cobalt blue and white paint with a little lemon yellow to create a pale blue, then mix the paint at a ratio of 2:3 with block-printing medium. Mix thoroughly with a hog-hair paintbrush and leave for a few minutes to get tacky.

5. Ink up template 1

Using the foam roller, roll up a little ink onto the old plate or chopping mat. The ink should sound wispy as you roll it, rather than sticky. Lightly roll the ink over the image so that it is evenly covered. **(b)**

6. Print template 1

Gripping the block at opposite ends, hold it in position above the paper to make sure that it will be centered with a slightly deeper border at the bottom edge of the paper than at the top. Place the block, ink-side down, onto the paper. Without shifting the block, place the palm of your hand on top and carefully apply pressure, lifting and repositioning your palm to make sure that all areas of the block have received the same amount of pressure.

Alternatively you can carefully roll a brayer over the back of the block, applying a little pressure as you roll, which applies even pressure over the whole of the block. Once you have printed off several prints, wash off the ink and thoroughly dry the block as well as cleaning and drying the inking-up station and roller.

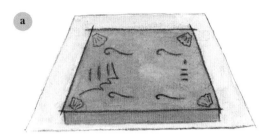

7. Trace and transfer template 2

Trace the Little boat 2 template on page 138. To make things a little easier when cutting out the design, colour the dark areas of the template in with pencil on your tracing so that they will be transferred onto the block. Line up the template with the edges of the block and the carved image, and transfer the image onto the block – be careful not to smudge the dark areas of pencil on the block once you've transferred them.

8. Cut out template 2 and mix ink

Using the No. 1 V lino-cutter, cut out all the unpencilled areas of the block (the exposed pink of the Speedy-Carve). Remember to carve away from a design to avoid cutting into it. For large areas use the No. 2 U lino-cutter. Once template 2 is cut, mix black and white paint with a little cobalt blue to make a dark blue-grey, then mix the paint at a ratio of 2:3 with block-printing medium. Mix thoroughly and leave for a few minutes to get tacky.

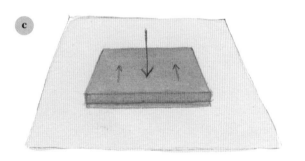

9. Print template 2

Roll up the ink (it should sound wispy as you roll it, rather than sticky), and evenly roll up the block. Place the blue print the right way up at the printing station. Holding the block at opposite ends and making sure that it is the right way up, position it above the pale blue printed image so that it is lined up with the edges and place it down onto the print. (c) Press down on the block using the palm of your hand, or carefully roll a brayer over the back of it, applying an even pressure as you roll over the whole of the block. (d) Remove the block by carefully lifting it up, one corner first. Repeat the process on the rest of the prints. Allow two to three hours for the prints to dry.

SONGTHRUSH CARD
two-colour polystyrene printing

I have very fond memories of running a printing project – both with my local Brownie group and with primary school children – using this polystyrene block-printing technique; they produced the most beautiful Christmas cards and prints. Even though the technique has its limitations, it's a great entry-level method of printing as it doesn't require any sophisticated tools or printing equipment to make great prints and cards. If you're trying to be thrifty, save the polystyrene disc that's used as backing for ready-made pizzas and use it for this project. For larger prints, Quickprint foam sheets can be easily sourced.

TIP

Remove any rings before starting this project as they can indent the polystyrene as you print.

YOU WILL NEED

Tracing paper

Black marker pen

Red, blue or green oil crayon

Masking tape or sticky tape

11.5 x 15cm (4½ x 6in) piece of thin, smooth polystyrene

5H pencil, blunt

Kebab skewer

Scalpel (X-Acto knife) fitted with 10A blade, or craft knife

Cutting mat

Newspaper

Newsprint

16.5 x 22cm (6⅓ x 8½in) card blanks or medium- to heavy-weight cartridge paper or white card cut to 33 x 22cm (13 x 8½in) and folded to give cards measuring 16.5 x 22cm (6⅓ x 8½in). These are large cards that can be wrapped up for sending in decorative wrapping paper

Soft-bodied acrylic paint – crimson, cobalt blue, lemon yellow and white

2 round-headed bristle paintbrushes

Block-printing or acrylic-printing medium

Old plate or chopping mat, for mixing paint – you may prefer to use 2, as 2 colours are mixed for this project

2 sponge rollers

Kitchen paper

LEVEL

Easy

TEMPLATES

Songthrush (see inside front cover), enlarged by 141%

METHOD

1. Trace and transfer the template

Enlarge the Songthrush template on the inside front cover then trace it onto tracing paper with black marker pen. Allow the pen to dry, then colour over the entire design with thick oil crayon. **(a)** Turn the tracing paper over and secure it with tape, crayon-side down, on the smooth polystyrene surface. With a blunt 5H pencil, trace over the dark lines of the image so that the design is transferred onto the surface of the polystyrene. The line should be firm but not so hard that the pencil pierces the polystyrene.

a

b

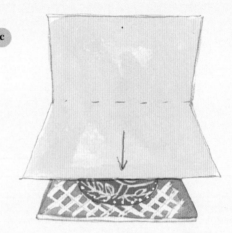

c

2. Impress and cut out the design

Remove the tracing paper and, with the 5H pencil, draw into the crayoned image on the polystyrene. (You might find that the polystyrene has a kind of "grain" or "resistance" that can cause the pencil to split the polystyrene and spoil the line. To stop this from happening, either go over the lines gently several times as you draw, or draw with the pencil held at an acute angle.) Note that the polystyrene is quite sensitive to pressure, so avoid pressing into it (with your fingernails, for example) as these indentations will appear on your print. Pierce the polystyrene with the point of a kebab skewer to create the dot details. Once you have drawn out the design, use a scalpel or craft knife on a cutting mat to carefully cut out the central oval shape, then pop this out gently.

3. Prepare the printing area

Place a few sheets of newspaper onto a flat work surface next to where your ink will be rolled out; this will be the inking-up station. Place a piece of newsprint onto a flat, clean area where you are going to print, along with your cartridge paper or white card, so that the two areas are separate from each other.

4. Prepare the printing inks and plate

For the card's pale blue background, mix cobalt blue and white paint with a little lemon yellow, then mix the paint at a ratio of 2:3 with block-printing or acrylic-printing medium. For the card's soft red centre, mix crimson and white paint with a little lemon yellow, then mix the paint at a ratio of 2:3 with block-printing or acrylic-printing medium. Mix each ink thoroughly with a hog-hair paintbrush. Roll one sponge roller in soft red paint and roll over the oval centre of polystyrene with an even coat of ink, taking care to make sure the paint is not too thick as it will fill in the design. Roll the second sponge roller in pale blue paint and roll over the rectangular polystyrene frame; place this in the printing area. Carefully place the inked-up oval centre of polystyrene back into the pale blue frame by dropping the oval in place and pushing its edges in **(b)** – try not to disturb the inked up surface too much, or mix the two colours.

5. Print the design

Place the bottom, landscape half of your card over the polystyrene printing plate so that the plate is positioned centrally on the bottom half of the card. **(c)** Hold the card firmly in place, and smooth over the whole of the polystyrene plate area (which you should be able feel under the card) with even pressure from the palm of your hand. Remove the card and place it on a flat, clean surface to dry. Gently take the polystyrene plate apart, ink it up again and continue to print as many cards as you need. If the image fills in with ink, carefully wash the polystyrene and dry it thoroughly with kitchen paper then resume printing. Once you have finished printing wash the inked up surfaces, rollers and plate and dry thoroughly with kitchen paper.

TOPIARY GARDEN PRINT
blended-colour polystyrene printing

This simple garden design demonstrates how you can make large, effective prints by "rolling up" a polystyrene printing plate with various colours. The beauty of this material is that you do not need a large printing press to print with it – just a pair of hands! For this project I have used a sheet of Quickprint foam, but the design could be adapted to fit a large round polystyrene pizza disc!

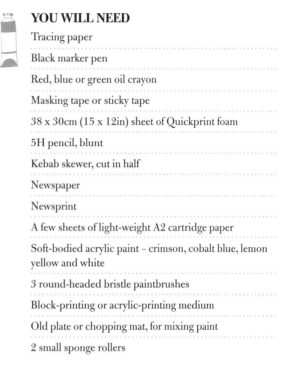

YOU WILL NEED

Tracing paper

Black marker pen

Red, blue or green oil crayon

Masking tape or sticky tape

38 x 30cm (15 x 12in) sheet of Quickprint foam

5H pencil, blunt

Kebab skewer, cut in half

Newspaper

Newsprint

A few sheets of light-weight A2 cartridge paper

Soft-bodied acrylic paint – crimson, cobalt blue, lemon yellow and white

3 round-headed bristle paintbrushes

Block-printing or acrylic-printing medium

Old plate or chopping mat, for mixing paint

2 small sponge rollers

LEVEL
Easy

TEMPLATES
Topiary garden (see page 139), enlarged by 141%

METHOD

1. Trace and transfer the template

Enlarge the Topiary garden template on page 139 then trace onto tracing paper with black marker pen. Once dy dry, colour over the design with thick oil crayon. **(a)** Turn the tracing paper over and secure with tape on the smooth polystyrene surface. With a blunt 5H pencil, trace over the dark lines of the image so that the design is transferred onto the surface of the polystyrene. The line should be firm but not so hard that the pencil pierces the polystyrene.

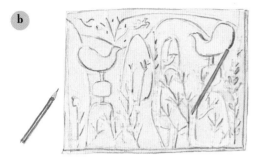

2. Impress the design into the polystyrene

Remove the tracing paper and, with the 5H pencil, draw into the crayoned image on the polystyrene, going over lines to make them thicker. To make the really thick lines for the topiary, use the blunt end of a kebab skewer that has been cut in half, instead of the pencil. **(b)**

3. Prepare the printing area

Place sheets of newspaper onto a flat work surface next to where your ink will be rolled out; this will be the inking-up station. Place a piece of newsprint onto a flat, clean area where you are going to print, along with your cartridge paper, so that the two areas are separate from each other.

4. Prepare the printing inks

For the dark green ink, mix cobalt blue and lemon yellow with a little white, then mix the paint at a ratio of 2:3 with block-printing or acrylic-printing medium. For the purple ink, mix crimson and cobalt blue with a little white, then mix 2:3 with block-printing or acrylic-printing medium. For the pale lilac ink, mix crimson and cobalt blue with white, then mix 2:3 with block-printing or acrylic-printing medium. Mix each ink thoroughly with a hog-hair paintbrush. If it dries out too quickly, add a little water.

5. Ink up the polystyrene printing plate

Place the polystyrene plate in the inking-up station and roll up the plate with dark green ink using the large sponge roller. This is a large plate so be careful when rolling it up with ink: try not to dent the plate with the edge of the roller as the indentation will end up in the print!

Once you have rolled the plate evenly with dark green ink, roll the bottom and top of the plate, and the areas in between the bases of the topiary, with pale lilac ink. You will notice that the roller will turn a lilac green; don't worry, this helps the ink to blend into the image so that there aren't too many hard lines of colour. To create the shadows, use a small roller and roll purple ink on the right-hand sides of the topiary – this is where you can play around a little with the colours, going over specific areas to strengthen them. **(c)** When you are happy with the image on the plate, lay it on the newsprint in the printing area, paint facing up.

6. Print the design

With clean hands, take the cartridge paper by its two opposite corners. Hold it above the plate and position it so that the plate will print centrally on the paper. When you are happy with the position of the paper, lower it onto the plate. Smooth over the whole of the plate area (which you should be able to feel under the paper) with even pressure from the palm of your hand. (Be careful not to shift the paper on the plate as you do this.) When you think that the image is printed (you can often see the shadow of the print on the back of the paper), gently peel one corner of the paper off the plate to check that it has printed properly. If it hasn't, replace the corner and apply more pressure to the plate. When you are happy that it is printed, carefully remove the paper from the plate. Because the paper is thin, it may have stuck itself to the plate, so remove it very gently. Allow the print to dry. Continue to roll up the plate with ink in the same way to print further pictures.

SCREEN-PRINTING

I used to think that screen-printing was an expensive, complicated process – but I have since realized that it doesn't have to be!

In this chapter I introduce you to a cheap and effective method of screen-printing, using regular as well as unconventional materials and equipment, so that you can produce multiple T-shirts, cards and simple textiles.

To keep the overall costs down you will need to source materials carefully. It is only worth using unconventional equipment if it is cheaper than the real thing – for example the window squeegee that I used was a quarter of the price of a proper screen-printing squeegee. DIY stores are a great place to source some of the materials.

PREPARING YOUR SCREEN

HOME-MADE PRINTING SCREEN

For the screen

Deep-edged canvas approx. 40 x 50cm (16 x 20in)

Pliers

Old table knife

Approx. 1m (1yd) white/cream matt polyester organza (not nylon, as it stretches)

Scissors

Light-duty staple gun with 6mm (¼in) staples

EQUIPMENT AND PAINT

If you are new to screen-printing there are a few things you should know about the equipment and materials that are involved.

- The deep-edged canvas is only needed for its frame, so the canvas quality is not important – you'll be taking it off anyway.

- Make sure that no image you plan to use is wider than the squeegee, as you must be able to pass over the whole image in one action.

- For paper-printing, any soft-bodied acrylic can be mixed 1:1 with textile medium so that it remains "open" on the screen (meaning that it will not block the fine mesh of the screen or dry out too quickly). Alternatively, you can use an acrylic printing medium purely for paper-printing.

- For fabric-printing, it's possible to achieve very good results using the same mixture of paint and acrylic textile medium as used for paper, but I recommend that you allow two to three weeks for the paint to dry completely, and then hand-wash only.

- For printing onto fabrics that will need to endure frequent washing – for example, tea towels – use fabric screen-printing inks. Use acrylic paint with a corresponding acrylic textile medium if you are prepared to hand-wash.

- When you are mixing up colours for printing, make sure that you have enough colour for an entire printing session; I tend to mix a little more than I need if I am mixing a specific colour. If you have any colour left over, put it in an airtight plastic container (a yogurt pot with plastic wrap over the top will work) and it will keep for a few weeks.

- There are several kinds of screen drawing fluid on the market. All of these will work with all liquid screen-fillers/blocks.

- There several kinds of screen-filler/block on the market. Some require screen-cleaner to clean them, some wash off with cream cleaner and water.

PREPARING YOUR SCREEN

1. Remove the canvas from its frame

Rip the canvas off of its frame and remove any remaining staples from the frame with pliers, while taking care to avoid any staples that may be holding the frame together. Use an old table knife for removing staples, loosening them with a levering action.

2. Prepare the organza

Cut the organza 8–10cm (3¼–4in) wider than the frame. Now attach the organza to the outside of the frame, ensuring that, if the frame has an angled edge on one side, you attach the organza to the opposite, flat side. To do this, stand the frame upright on a flat surface and lay the organza over the top edge, making sure that the edge of the organza is level with the frame edge, and that you have an equal border of 4–5cm (1½–2in) all the way around.

3. Staple the organza to the frame

Starting from the middle of the top edge of the frame, staple the organza to the frame. **(a)** Staple either side of the middle staple, then towards each corner – using around five staples in total. Rotate the frame by 180 degrees and staple the organza to the bottom edge of the

frame, pulling the organza taut as you staple. Next turn the frame on its side and staple the organza to the side of the frame in the same way, pulling the organza taut as you staple. When stapling the final side of the frame pull the organza really tight – but be careful not to rip it.

4. Check and finish the frame

It is important that the organza is taut, like the surface of a drum, on the frame as this can affect printed results. Check the frame for loose fabric, pull this and staple it tight, and then fold all four corners of organza over and staple it neatly to the corners of the frame. **(b and c)**

5. Before you start printing

Once your screen is prepared you should familiarize yourself with the printing process before you start any serious projects. Play around with stencils and the drawing fluid using different paintbrushes to see what kind of marks and effects you can get. It is also useful to practise applying screen-filler/block to your screen. For each new project, print a few test paper prints to check that everything is printing correctly before you print onto the surface of your project.

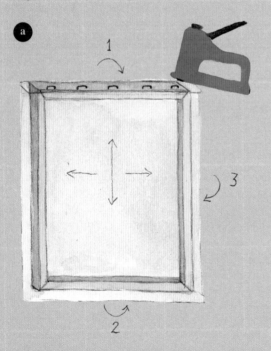

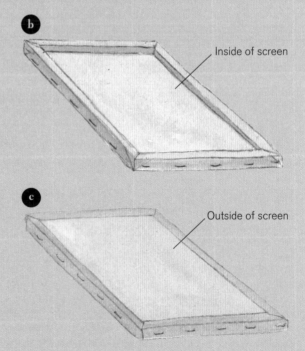

Inside of screen

Outside of screen

HEN TEA TOWEL
screen-printing with a stencil

This cheap and effective introduction to screen-printing uses a stencil, so there's no need for screen-filler/block or drawing fluid. Cut stencils are simple and stylish, and although stencils used in screen-printing were traditionally made from paper, I have found that repositional book-covering film makes a more durable, reliable stencil and is also more economical with paint. It might be worth trying out very simple designs, such as an apple or numbers, to familiarize yourself with the process before starting on this project.

YOU WILL NEED

A3 sheet of tracing paper

3B pencil

5H pencil

A3-sized piece clear repositional book-covering film

Scalpel (X-Acto knife) fitted with 10A blade, or craft knife

Cutting mat

Home-made 40 x 50cm (16 x 20in) printing screen (see pages 96–98)

Masking tape

Newspaper

Newsprint

Cotton/linen tea towels, prepared for printing (see page 11)

Soft-bodied acrylic paint – crimson and yellow; or fabric screen-printing ink that can withstand machine washing – cadmium red

Acrylic textile medium (if using acrylic paints)

A round-headed bristle paintbrush

Old jam jar or yogurt pot, for mixing paint

Cartridge paper

Old dessert spoon

Large window squeegee roughly 35cm (14in) wide

Iron and ironing board

Kitchen paper

LEVEL
Intermediate

TEMPLATES
Hen (see inside back cover), enlarged by 200%

TIP
Very good results can be obtained using soft-bodied acrylic mixed with textile medium, but do allow two to three weeks for the paint to dry, and only ever hand-wash these tea towels.

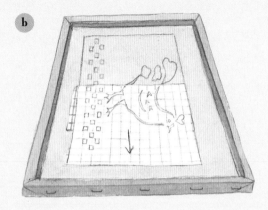

METHOD

1. Trace the design

Enlarge the Hen template on the inside back cover, then trace and transfer the design onto the tracing paper (see page 10), extending the template's checkered pattern to fit the width of your tea towels, but leaving a 1cm (½in) border on the tracing paper either side of the checkered pattern. Centre the traced image on the paper backing of the book-covering film, allowing a border all the way round the image and transfer the design.

2. Cut out the design

Cut out the stencil using a sharp scalpel or craft knife on a cutting mat; extra care and concentration is needed when cutting the stencil to ensure that you cut within the traced lines (any cuts beyond the lines could let ink through when you are printing). **(a)**

3. Stick the stencil to the screen

Once the stencil is cut, check that it fits centrally on the inside of the screen with edge borders of 2.5cm (1in) or more. Place the prepared screen face-down on a flat, clean surface. Take the stencil and peel about 2.5cm (1in) of the backing paper away, then align the top edge centrally on the inside of the screen and stick it down. Gently peel back the remaining backing paper **(b)**, smoothing the stencil down lightly as you go. The book-covering film has a tendency to curl, so peel the backing off slowly and, if there are any wrinkles in it, lift and reposition the film carefully. Once you are satisfied

with the placement of the stencil, smooth down the book-covering film firmly onto the screen. Check to see that it is flat under a bright light, flattening any undulations (any wrinkles will let the ink through and spoil the design).

4. Mask the screen

Apply long strips of masking tape along each side of the stencil, from the stencil's edges to your screen's frame, filling the space between the stencil and the frame and folding the tape at right-angles to seal it to the wood. **(c)** Then turn the screen over and mask the outer edges of the screen to prevent ink seeping through when you print.

5. Prepare the printing area

Lay a few sheets of newspaper on a flat, level work surface, such as a kitchen table, sticking them in place with masking tape to protect the surface. Depending on how many tea towels you are printing, trim several sheets of newsprint to the size of your tea towels – these will prevent ink from transferring from the towels to other surfaces. Lay the first prepared tea towel right-side up on top of a piece of trimmed newsprint and lay both the towel and the newsprint in a landscape position on the work surface, smoothing out any wrinkles with the palms of your hands. Create registration marks on the newspaper by marking out the tea towel's edges with a pencil or masking tape. Position the printing screen face-down on top of the tea towel, in a portrait position, so that the design is 2.5–4cm (1–1½in) from the bottom edge of the tea towel with an

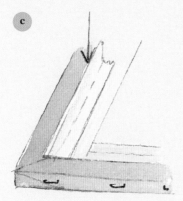

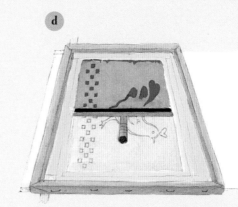

even space at each end of the checkered pattern. Create further registration marks on the newspaper by marking out the screen's edges with a pencil or masking tape.

6. Prepare the printing inks

If using acrylic paint, create a cadmium red by mixing crimson and lemon yellow. Mix the colour with a similar volume of acrylic textile medium.

7. Take a proof print

It is worth taking a proof print on cartridge paper first to check that everything is printing correctly. Once you have created registration marks for printing, remove the tea towel and replace it with a sheet of paper. Take a proof print by following the printing instructions in step 8. Once you are happy with the image, print your tea towels.

8. Print the image

Spoon your chosen ink onto the inside of the printing screen, 2.5cm (1in) above the top of the image so that it creates a rectangular pool about 2.5cm (1in) deep and as wide as the width of the image. With one hand, press down the top edge of the screen. Position the squeegee behind the ink so that it will pass over the whole of the image. Pull the squeegee towards you, pulling the ink over the stencil (as if you were cleaning a window). **(d)** When you get to the bottom of the screen, check to ensure that the entire image has been printed by looking closely at the screen. If it has not, add a little more ink to the top of the screen

and repeat the process. Lift the squeegee off the screen, transferring any ink from the edge of the squeegee into your jam jar or yogurt pot, and rest the squeegee on its back on the newspaper, well away from the tea towel.

9. Lift the screen

Gently lift the screen up and rest it against something, making sure that it is not dripping with ink. Carefully lift up the tea towel and the newsprint backing paper, and lay these on a flat surface to dry. Be careful not to let the fabric of the tea towel fall onto itself as ink from the design can be transferred to other parts of the fabric. Repeat the printing process as desired; you should be able to print up to 20 tea towels from the same screen. If you do find some ink creeping through the stencil, turn the screen around and pull the ink the other way, out of any undulations. Do this on a separate piece of paper to clear the screen, then continue printing this way around on the opposite end of the tea towel. Once the prints are dry, heat-set the ink with a medium iron (see page 11).

10. Clean up

Once you have finished printing remove the masking tape and stencil from the screen and clean the screen and squeegee – I find this is best done in the bath, using a shower attachment, but be sure to clean the bath immediately after washing the screen to avoid staining. Dry the screen with kitchen paper or leave to dry outside if it's a dry day.

BLUEBIRD DRAWSTRING BAG
screen-printing with a stencil & wax resist

This is an easy and effective way of printing – and it's something that children can get involved with. The technique combines a stencil with a wax drawing, which will act as a resist to the ink. The results are quite eyecatching – the bluebird looks as if it has been appliquéd onto the fabric.

I have designed a simple bird silhouette for this project, but you could create all kinds of simple designs using the same technique, for example stars, flower heads, fruit, boats and planes.

The most important things to remember with this technique are to make sure that the stencil is well adhered to the screen, and that the wax drawing is solid and fills in the mesh of the screen to create a proper resist.

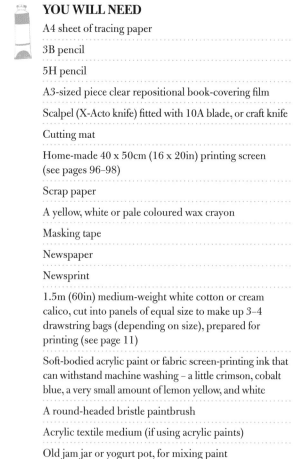

YOU WILL NEED
A4 sheet of tracing paper

3B pencil

5H pencil

A3-sized piece clear repositional book-covering film

Scalpel (X-Acto knife) fitted with 10A blade, or craft knife

Cutting mat

Home-made 40 x 50cm (16 x 20in) printing screen (see pages 96–98)

Scrap paper

A yellow, white or pale coloured wax crayon

Masking tape

Newspaper

Newsprint

1.5m (60in) medium-weight white cotton or cream calico, cut into panels of equal size to make up 3–4 drawstring bags (depending on size), prepared for printing (see page 11)

Soft-bodied acrylic paint or fabric screen-printing ink that can withstand machine washing – a little crimson, cobalt blue, a very small amount of lemon yellow, and white

A round-headed bristle paintbrush

Acrylic textile medium (if using acrylic paints)

Old jam jar or yogurt pot, for mixing paint

Cartridge paper

Large window squeegee, at least 16cm (6¼in) wide

Old dessert spoon

Iron and ironing board

Kitchen paper

Sewing machine and thread

LEVEL
Easy

TEMPLATE
Bluebird (see page 134), enlarged by 200%

METHOD

1. Trace the design

Enlarge the Bluebird template on page 134, then trace and transfer the design centrally onto the paper backing of the book-covering film (see page 10).

2. Cut out the design

Cut out the bluebird using a sharp scalpel or craft knife on a cutting mat; extra care and concentration is needed when cutting the stencil to ensure that you cut within the traced lines (any cuts beyond the lines could let ink through when you are printing).

3. Stick the stencil to the screen

Once the stencil is cut, place the prepared screen face-down on a flat, clean surface. Take the stencil and peel about 2.5cm (1in) of the backing paper away, then align the top edge centrally on the inside of the screen and stick it down. Gently peel back the remaining backing paper, smoothing the stencil down lightly as you go. The book-covering film has a tendency to curl, so peel the backing off slowly and, if there are any wrinkles in it, lift and reposition the film carefully. Once you are satisfied with the placement of the stencil, smooth down the book-covering film firmly onto the screen. Check to see that it is flat under a bright light, flattening any undulations (any wrinkles will let the ink through and spoil the design).

4. Draw the flowers

Practise drawing a few simple flowers onto a piece of scrap paper using your crayon. When you feel confident, draw out the flowers on the exposed screen within the bird stencil. **(a)** Start by drawing a flower where the bird's eye will be, as the centre of the flower will represent the bird's eye. When you draw with the crayon, press very firmly as, to act effectively as a resist, the lines of wax must be thick. Be careful to not disturb the edge of the stencil. Follow the template drawing on page 134 as a rough guide as to where to position your flowers. Every so often, hold the screen up to the light to check that the lines of your flowers are not holey. If they are, go over them again. I find that it is easier to draw with the crayon if it is sharpened to a point.

5. Prepare the screen for printing

Once you have finished drawing out the flowers, brush off any flakes of crayon from the screen and work surface and make sure that the inner edges of the stencil are still firmly in place. Apply long strips of masking tape along each side of the stencil, from the stencil's edges to your screen's frame, filling the space between the stencil and the frame and folding the tape at right-angles to seal it to the wood. Then turn the screen over and mask the outer edges of screen to prevent ink seeping through when you print.

6. Prepare the printing area

Lay a few sheets of newspaper on a flat, level work surface, sticking them in place with masking tape. Depending on how many panels you are printing, trim several sheets of newsprint the size of your prepared panels – these will prevent ink from transferring from the panels to other surfaces. Lay the first panel right-side up on top of a piece of newsprint and lay both panel and newsprint horizontally on the work surface, smoothing out any wrinkles with the palms of your hands. Create registration marks on the newspaper by marking out the panel's edges with a pencil or masking tape. Position the screen face-down on top of the panel, in a portrait position, so that the design has a deep border at the bottom of the panel and an even border at the sides. Create further registration marks on the newspaper by marking out the screen's edges.

7. Prepare the printing inks

If using acrylic paint, create the sky blue colour by mixing a little crimson with cobalt blue and a very small amount of lemon yellow, and white paint. Mix the colour with a similar volume of acrylic textile medium.

8. Take a proof print

It is worth taking a proof print on cartridge paper first to check that everything is printing correctly. Once you have created the registration marks, remove the panel and replace it with a sheet of paper. Take a proof print by following the printing instructions in step 9. If the wax resist isn't strong enough, pass the squeegee over the

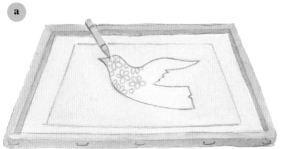

frame until as much of the ink is removed as possible without disturbing the image and go over any holey areas of the design with a wax crayon until they are covered. Once you are happy with the image, print your fabric.

9. Print the image

Spoon your chosen ink onto the inside of the printing screen, 2.5cm (1in) above the top of the image so that it creates a rectangular pool about 2.5cm (1in) deep and as wide as the width of the image. It is important that you have enough ink as you only want to have to travel over the image with the squeegee once for each print, as the resist might not hold. With one hand, press down the top edge of the screen. Position the squeegee behind the ink so that it will pass over the whole of the image. Pull the squeegee towards you, not too heavily, pulling the ink over the stencil. **(b)** If you find that some of the image has not printed you'll need to weigh the risks of going over the stencil one more time against filling in the design. If you decide to go over it again, put a little ink on the edge of the squeegee and lightly go over the area. Lift the squeegee off the screen, transferring any ink from the edge of the squeegee into your jam jar or yogurt pot, and rest the squeegee on its back on the newspaper.

10. Lift the screen

When you have finished printing, hold the corner of the fabric down as you lift up the screen gently because the fabric might have adhered itself to the screen. Gently lift

the screen up and rest it against something, making sure that it is not dripping with ink. Carefully lift up the fabric panel and the newsprint backing paper, and lay these on a flat surface to dry. Be careful not to let the panel fall onto itself as ink from the design can be transferred to other parts of the fabric. Repeat the printing process on a new panel of material. Once the prints are dry, heat-set the ink with a medium iron (see page 11).

11. Clean up

Once you have finished printing remove the masking tape and stencil from the screen and clean the screen and squeegee. Use a bathroom cream cleaner and a scouring sponge to clean off the crayon, being careful not to disturb the weave of the organza, and dry the screen with kitchen paper or leave to dry outside if it's a dry day.

12. Sew your bag

Hem the top edges of the two panels, pin together inside-out and sew together with a 1cm (½in) seam allowance. Turn the bag the right way round. Cut another fabric strip that's 6cm (2½in) deep and 5cm (2in) longer than the bag's circumference. Hem each edge of the strip and pin down 5cm (2in) from the top edge of the bag – this will be the channel for the ribbon. Sew the strip top and bottom, but leave it open at both side seams. Using a safety pin attached to 1m (1yd) of pink ribbon, thread it through the channel until it comes out the other end. Then tie the two ends together and trim the ribbon to a point.

COMPANION CAT CUSHION
screen-printing with drawing fluid

Drawing fluid is a great medium for creating images. You can be both precise and expressive in your painting and, because of the screen-filler/block's durability, you can print several images – and in various colours.

There is something about the combination of black and natural linen that really works for me. The simplicity of this cushion means that it will work with most interiors. I have printed onto pre-cut panels of linen that I have then made into envelope cushion covers; alternatively you can print this onto a ready-made cushion, tote bag or tea towel. You could also try it on a good-quality cartridge paper as a print for the wall – it would look great in a warm red or cerulean blue!

TIPS

If you find that the image doesn't print properly, you may need to place a few more sheets of paper under your fabric so that it is in closer contact with the printing screen.

YOU WILL NEED

Home-made 40 x 50cm (16 x 20in) printing screen (see pages 96–98)

3B pencil

Newsprint

A size 1 fine paintbrush

Screen drawing fluid

Liquid screen-filler/block

Large window squeegee roughly 35cm (14in) wide

A size 5 or medium pointed, round paintbrush

Masking tape

Steam iron and ironing board

Thick cardboard or paper cut to size to fit inside the cushion covers (if using ready-made cushions)

Soft-bodied acrylic paint or fabric screen-printing ink that can withstand machine washing – black

Acrylic textile medium (if using acrylic paints)

Newspaper

A length of natural linen, prepared for printing (see page 11). Depending on the size of your cushion pad, 50cm (20in) linen can work well to make one cushion. If you're not confident with a sewing machine, use ready-made cushion covers instead

Cartridge paper

Old dessert spoon

Old jam jar or yogurt pot, for mixing paint

Sewing machine and thread

LEVEL
Intermediate

TEMPLATES

Companion cat (see page 135), enlarged by 200%

a

b

METHOD

1. Trace the image

Enlarge the Companion cat template on page 135. Make sure that the organza is tight on the prepared screen, then place the screen face-down positioned centrally on top of the cat image. Trace around the cat with a 3B pencil onto the back of the screen's organza. **(a)**

2. Paint the image

Place a sheet of newsprint on your work surface and turn the frame over onto it; you should be able to see the pencil drawing on the outside of the organza. Using a fine paintbrush, paint the cat on the outside of the screen with screen drawing fluid; try not to lean on the organza as it could stretch. **(b)** Allow the image to dry for a few hours.

3. Apply screen-filler/block

Once the image is dry, shake the bottle of screen-filler/block and pour out a line of it about 2.5cm (1in) above the top of the image, so that it creates a rectangular pool about 2.5cm (1in) deep and 2.5cm (1in) wider than the width of the image on each side. Position the squeegee behind the screen-filler/block so that it will pass over the whole of the image when it is pulled over the screen. Pull the squeegee towards you in one action, pulling the screen-filler/block over the cat design **(c)** – do not go back over the image! You will probably have a residue of screen-filler/block at the sides; coax this into the outer areas of the screen that have not been covered. Allow the screen to dry in a flat position and wash the squeegee.

4. Remove the drawing fluid

Once the screen is thoroughly dry, wash off the drawing fluid with cool water (this is best done in the bath with a shower attachment) to reveal the cat image on the screen. Allow the screen to dry once more. Check the screen for any pinholes in the screen-filler/block by holding it up to the light; fill any holes by painting in with screen-filler/block using a medium paintbrush, then allow to dry again.

5. Prepare the screen for printing

Apply long strips of masking tape along each side of the screen-filler/block's edge, filling the space between the screen-filler/block and the frame and folding the tape at right-angles to seal it to the wood. Then turn the screen over and mask the outer edges of the screen to prevent ink seeping through when you print.

6. Prepare the fabric

Iron your fabric with a steam iron to ensure that all creases have been ironed out of the fabric before printing. If you are printing onto ready-made cushions, place a thick sheet of cardboard or paper – that has been cut to size to fit the interiors of the cushions – inside to prevent any ink seeping through the fabric when you print.

7. Prepare the printing inks

If using acrylic paint, mix black paint with a similar volume of acrylic textile medium. Alternatively you can use black fabric screen-printing ink.

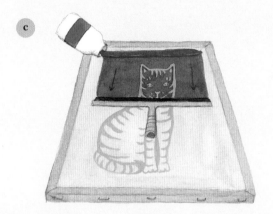

8. Prepare the printing area

Lay a few sheets of newspaper on a flat, level work surface, such as a kitchen table, sticking them in place with masking tape. Place your fabric or cushion cover right-side up on top of a sheet of trimmed newsprint, then lay both the fabric and the newsprint in portrait position on the work surface. Position your printing screen face-down on top of the fabric, in a portrait position, so that the design will print centrally. Create registration marks on the newspaper by marking out the screen and fabric edges with a pencil or masking tape.

9. Take a proof print

It is worth taking a proof print on cartridge paper first to check that everything is printing correctly. Once you have created registration marks for printing, remove the fabric and replace it with a sheet of paper. Take a proof print by following the printing instructions in step 10. Once you are happy with the image, print your cushion covers.

10. Print the image

Spoon your chosen ink onto the inside of the printing screen, 2.5cm (1in) above the top of the image so that it creates a rectangular pool about 2.5cm (1in) deep and as wide as the width of the image. With one hand, press down the top edge of the screen. Position the squeegee behind the ink so that it will pass over the whole of the image. Pull the squeegee towards you, pulling the ink over the stencil. **(d)** When you get to the bottom of the screen,

check to ensure that the entire image has been printed by looking closely at the screen. If you are not sure, you can gently lift up one corner of the screen (as long as you don't move the screen out of position) to see if the image has printed. If it has not, add a little more ink to the top of screen and repeat the process. Lift the squeegee off the screen, transferring any ink from the edge of the squeegee into your jam jar or yogurt pot, and rest the squeegee on its back on the newspaper, well away from the fabric or cushion cover.

11. Lift the screen

Hold the corner of the fabric down as you lift up the screen gently. Rest the screen against something, making sure that it is not dripping with ink. Carefully lift up the fabric and the newsprint backing paper, and lay these on a flat surface to dry. Repeat the process on a new piece of fabric using a fresh piece of newsprint. Once the prints are dry, heat-set the ink with a medium iron (see page 11).

12. Sew your cushion (if required)

If you have printed pieces of fabric, use a sewing machine to make it up into simple cushions.

13. Clean up

If you'd like to print the image in a different colourway, remove the tape from the screen and wash it out with cold water (this will remove the ink but not the screen-filler/block). Allow the screen to dry thoroughly before printing.

CHILDREN'S PARTY INVITATIONS
quilting hoop screen-printing with drawing fluid

I have always wanted to own a Gocco printer – a small, compact and completely self-contained Japanese colour screen-printing system – but these are now very difficult to come by. However, I like the idea of producing small prints in volume in a quick, easy and cost-effective way, so have come up with a comparable method of printing invitations and cards – and the results have a wonderful hand-made charm about them. One of the problems with some screen-fillers is that they are quite difficult to remove without chemical cleaners. But using a quilting hoop avoids the need for this because the fabric can be removed easily and agitated to help get it clean.

LEVEL
Easy

TEMPLATES
Kitty cat (see page 136), enlarged by 141%

YOU WILL NEED
40cm (16in) square white/cream matt polyester organza

30cm (12in) diameter quilting hoop

2B pencil

Newsprint

A6 card blanks, 15 x 11cm (6 x 4¼in) folded size to fit in C6 envelopes

Masking tape

Screen drawing fluid

Small dish

A size 1 fine paintbrush

Liquid screen-filler/block

Rubber grout squeegee, large squeegee for tiling or window squeegee – no wider than 20cm (8in)

A size 5 or medium pointed, round paintbrush

Soft-bodied acrylic paint – crimson, ultramarine blue, lemon yellow and white

Acrylic textile medium

Old dessert spoon

Old jam jar or yogurt pot, for mixing paint

Old table knife

C6 envelopes

METHOD

1. Trace the image
Enlarge the Kitty cat template on page 136. Place the square of organza into the quilting hoop, then tighten the bolt on the hoop while pulling any puckered or loose parts of the organza tight, like a drum. Place the quilting hoop face-down, positioned centrally on top of the cat design, so that the weave of the organza runs parallel to the design. Trace the cat design onto the organza with a soft 2B pencil. **(a)**

2. Prepare the printing area
Place a sheet of newsprint onto a flat, level work surface, such as a kitchen table, and position an opened-out card

a

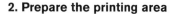

blank onto the newsprint, with the front of the card on the right-hand side. Create registration marks on the newsprint by marking out the card's corners with masking tape. Position the quilting hoop on top of the card blank so that the cat design is positioned centrally on the card front. Create further registration marks on the newsprint by drawing around the hoop with a pencil. **(b)**

3. Paint the design

Turn the quilting hoop over so that the outside is facing up. Pour a little drawing fluid into a dish. Dip a fine paintbrush into the fluid, and paint off any excess into the dish. With a steady hand, paint the drawn image with drawing fluid; try not to lean on the organza as it could stretch. Go over any parts of the image that are thin or holey. **(c)** Allow to dry.

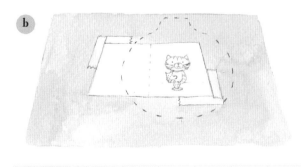

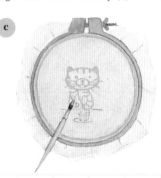

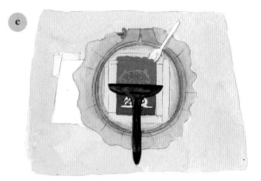

4. Apply screen-filler/block

Once the image is dry, shake the bottle of screen-filler/block and pour out a line of it about 2.5cm (1in) above the top of the image, so that it creates a rectangular pool about 2.5cm (1in) deep and 2.5cm (1in) wider than the width of the image on each side. Position the squeegee behind the screen-filler/block so that it will pass over the whole of the image when it is pulled over the screen. Pull the squeegee towards you in one action, pulling the screen-filler/block over the cat design. **(d)** Try to do this in one action, as it is important not to go back over the image. You will probably have a residue of screen-filler/block at the sides; coax this into the outer areas of the screen that have not been covered, making sure that you do not come in contact with any of the central image – if there is too much it could cover up the drawing fluid. Allow the screen to dry in a flat position and wash the squeegee.

5. Remove the drawing fluid

Once your screen is thoroughly dry, wash off the drawing fluid with cool water (this is best done in the bath with a shower attachment) to reveal the cat image on the screen. Allow the screen to dry once more. Check the screen for any pinholes in the screen-filler/block by holding it up to the light; fill any holes by painting in with screen-filler/block using a medium paintbrush, then allow to dry again.

6. Prepare the screen for printing

With masking tape mask off a wide border along each side of the image to prevent ink seepage when printing. Do the same to mask the other side of the screen.

7. Prepare the printing inks

Create orange by mixing crimson paint with lemon yellow and a little white. Create green by mixing ultramarine blue paint with lemon yellow and a little white. Add a similar volume of acrylic textile medium to each colour.

8. Print the image

Position a blank card within the registration marks on the newsprint, then position the quilting hoop face-down on top of the card. Spoon ink onto the inside of the printing screen, 2.5cm (1in) above the top of the image so that it creates a rectangular pool about 2.5cm (1in) deep and as wide as the width of the image. Hold the hoop firmly in place with one hand and with the other hand gently pull the ink over the image with the squeegee. **(e)** Lift the hoop, remove the card, replace with the next card and repeat the process. If the image is not completely printed, you may need more ink. If the image is smudged, you may have applied too much pressure to the squeegee. If too much ink gathers at the bottom of the hoop, scrape it off with a table knife and transfer it to the top of hoop. Print as many cards as required. If the image starts to fill in, wash the screen thoroughly, remove and replace the masking tape once screen is dry, then resume printing.

9. Clean up

To clean the organza remove it from the hoop, then place it in warm, soapy water to soak, agitating it intermittently to remove the ink and screen-filler/block. Rinse and allow to dry. Once the cards have dried, write your message in them and place into C6 envelopes ready to send.

AEROPLANE T-SHIRT
three-colour screen-printing

Screen-printing is often associated with bold, graphic images. I printed this fun T-shirt for my son, who loves to make model aeroplanes. This is a great way of printing a batch of T-shirts with the same logo.

This project teaches how to build up an image, combining the white background of the T-shirt with three printed colours. You will see how different screen-printing processes can be combined to create an image.

YOU WILL NEED

Home-made 40 x 50cm (16 x 20in) printing screen (see pages 96–98)

Permanent marker pen

3B pencil

5H pencil

A3 tracing paper

A3-sized piece clear repositional book-covering film

Scalpel (X-Acto knife) fitted with 10A blade

Cutting mat

Masking tape

Thick cardboard or paper cut to size to fit inside T-shirt

Newsprint

Plain white T-shirts, prepared for printing (see page 11)

Soft-bodied acrylic paint or fabric screen-printing ink that can withstand machine washing – crimson, ultramarine blue, lemon yellow, black and white

Acrylic textile medium

Old dessert spoon

Old jam jar or yogurt pot, for mixing paint

Large window squeegee, roughly 35cm (14in) wide

Kitchen paper

A size 5 medium paintbrush

Screen drawing fluid

Small dish

Liquid screen-filler/block

Iron and ironing board

LEVEL

Intermediate

TEMPLATES

Aeroplane (see page 136), enlarged by 141%

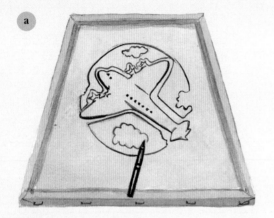

a

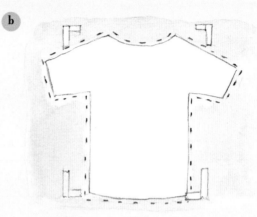

b

METHOD

1. Trace the image

Enlarge the Aeroplane template on page 136. Place the printing screen face-down, positioned centrally on top of the aeroplane design, and trace the design onto the organza using a permanent marker pen. **(a)** Include the outline of every shape, no matter what its colour. You will only be able to use the organza once but this will ensure that your colour separations are properly registered.

2. Print the first colour

Trace the first colour separation – the light grey body of the aeroplane – and transfer it to the paper backing of the book-covering film (see page 10). Carefully cut out the stencil using a scalpel on a cutting mat, then place it onto the inside of screen, backing-side down, lining up the cut-out shape with the marked image on the screen. Once in position, carefully peel off a corner of the backing and stick it down to hold the position, then peel off the rest of the backing, sticking the template firmly in place as you go. Apply long strips of masking tape along each side of the book-covering film, from the film's edges to your screen's frame, filling the space between the film and the frame and folding the tape at right-angles to seal it to the wood. **(c)** Then turn the screen over and mask the outer edges of the screen to prevent ink seeping through when you print. Place a thick sheet of cardboard or paper – that has been cut to size to fit the T-shirt – inside to prevent

any ink seeping through the fabric when you print. Tape newsprint to your work surface, lay the T-shirt onto the surface and mark its outline with a pencil. Place the printing screen face-down on top of the T-shirt, so that the aeroplane is positioned centrally on the T-shirt and create registration marks on the newsprint by marking out the edges of the screen with masking tape. **(b)** Create a light grey ink by mixing white paint with a little black, ultramarine blue and lemon yellow. Mix thoroughly with a similar volume of acrylic textile medium. Spoon the ink onto the back of the printing screen, 2.5cm (1in) above the top of the image so that it creates a rectangular pool about 2.5cm (1in) deep and as wide as the width of the image. Position the squeegee behind the ink so that it will pass over the whole of the image when it is pulled over the screen. Pull the squeegee towards you in one action, pulling the ink over the design. **(c)** Carefully lift the screen, then repeat the process on the next T-shirt if you are printing more than one. Allow the T-shirts to dry.

3. Clean the screen

Remove the masking tape and stencil from the screen and wash it thoroughly in the bath with a shower attachment, being careful not to shower watery ink everywhere. Clean the bath immediately after washing the screen as the ink may stain the bath if is left to dry. Dry the screen with kitchen paper or leave it to dry outside if it's a dry day.

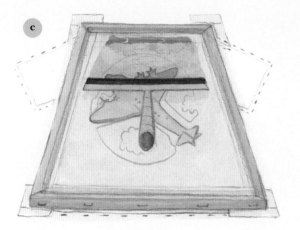

4. Print the second colour

Paint the second colour separation – the dark grey outline of the plane – onto the outside of the printing screen with drawing fluid and a medium paintbrush, using the template as a guide. Once the image is dry, shake the bottle of screen-filler/block and pour out a line of it about 2.5cm (1in) above the top of the image, so that it creates a rectangular pool about 2.5cm (1in) deep and 2.5cm (1in) wider than the width of the image on each side. Position the squeegee behind the screen-filler/block so that it will pass over the whole image when it is pulled over the screen. Pull the squeegee towards you in one action, pulling the screen-filler/block over the design – do not go back over the image! You will probably have a residue of screen-filler/block at the sides; coax this into the outer areas of the screen that have not been covered. Allow the screen to dry in a flat position and wash the squeegee. When the screen is dry, wash out the drawing fluid (this is best done in the bath with a shower attachment) to reveal the aeroplane image on the screen. Allow the screen to dry once more, then fill any pinholes with screen-filler/block. With masking tape mask off a wide border along each side of the image on both sides of the screen (see step 5, page 108). Create a dark grey ink by mixing ultramarine blue, black and white paint thoroughly with a similar volume of acrylic textile medium. Use the registration marks on the newsprint to line up the first T-shirt, and then line up the printing screen in the same way. (You should be able to see through the screen to double-check that it is lined up with the first printed image.) Print the second colour onto the T-shirts using the same method as in step 2. Depending on what screen-filler/block you have used, clean this off the screen in the appropriate way so that just the marker pen outline remains.

5. Print the third colour

Paint the third colour separation – the yellow sky – onto the outside of the printing screen with drawing fluid, stippling the edges of the clouds with a dry brush **(d)** and repeat the preparation process using screen-filler/block as described in step 4. Create a warm yellow ink by mixing lemon yellow paint with white and a touch of crimson. Mix thoroughly with a similar volume of acrylic textile medium. Line the screen up with the printed image and registration marks and print as described in step 2. Allow the T-shirt to dry. Once the print is dry, heat-set the ink with a medium iron (see page 11).

6. Clean up

To clean the screen and squeegee, place them in warm, soapy water to soak, agitating them intermittently to remove the ink. Remove the screen-filler/block with the appropriate cleaner. Rinse and allow to dry.

BUTTERFLY-CHARMER SCARF
photo emulsion screen-printing

Photo emulsion screen-printing is a magical way of achieving fine lines and details in a screen-print. There is a cost to this way of working, as you will need to invest in a photo emulsion screen-printing kit but, depending on the size of your screen and your image, you should be able to make several images with it.

This method of printing can be used to print all kinds of items, from cards and flyers to tote bags and T-shirts, and it is particularly good for printing images with type on. It can also be combined with two or more screen processes and colours, or used to create an image with a greater depth, as fine lines and small details are often the elements that can pull an image together.

You can find plain silk scarves and handkerchiefs online or at specialist craft shops. The scarf I chose was long and fairly narrow, which works very well with the design.

TIP

If you do not have a printer (or access to one), a copy shop should be able to photocopy your chosen image onto transparent film.

YOU WILL NEED

Scanner and printer, or photocopier

Acetate sheet compatible with printer

Fine marker pen

Rubber gloves

Apron

Photo emulsion solution for screen-printing

Newspaper

Hairdryer with a cool setting

Home-made 40 x 50cm (16 x 20in) printing screen (see pages 96–98)

Large window squeegee, roughly 35cm (14in) wide

Sticky tape

Clear glass, slightly larger than the image

Anglepoise lamp with 100-watt clear/incandescent bulb

Stencil brush

Liquid screen-filler/block

A size 5 or medium pointed, round paintbrush

Masking tape

Cartridge paper

Newsprint

Ponge 5 silk scarf, 35 x 130cm (14 x 51in)

Soft-bodied acrylic paint or fabric screen-printing ink that can withstand machine washing – black

Acrylic textile medium (if using acrylic paints)

Old dessert spoon

Old jam jar or yogurt pot, for mixing paint

An extra pair of hands

Iron and ironing board

LEVEL

Intermediate

TEMPLATES

Butterfly charmer (see page 134), enlarged by 141%

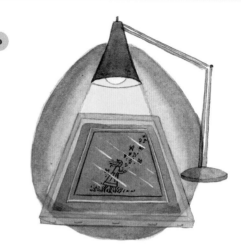

METHOD

1. Prepare the positive artwork

Enlarge the Butterfly charmer template on page 134. Either scan and print or photocopy the template artwork onto acetate that is compatible with your particular printer. Make sure that the image is truly black and white by adjusting the brightness/contrast of the image on your computer or copier before printing. When you print the image, make sure that the "simulate paper colour" option is turned off. Alternatively, you could draw your own design directly onto acetate with a fine marker pen.

2. Prepare the printing area

Wearing rubber gloves and an apron, follow the manufacturer's instructions for mixing up the photo emulsion solution. (Store any unused solution in its bottle in a plastic bag in the fridge; it should keep for up to four months.) Work in a well-ventilated, darkened room (a room with heavy curtains or shutters should do), but make sure there is enough light for you to see. Cover a work surface with newspaper and have a hairdryer to hand.

3. Coat the screen

Pour a line of photo emulsion solution along the top edge of the outside of your printing screen, so that it creates a rectangular pool about 2.5cm (1in) deep and as wide as the width of the screen. Position the squeegee behind the photo emulsion solution and pull the squeegee towards

you in one action, pulling the solution over the whole of the screen **(a)** – do not go back over the screen unless the solution is too thick or there are air bubbles. (If the coating is too thick it will come away in places when you wash out the image). You will probably have a residue of solution at the sides; coax this into the outer areas of the screen that have not been covered and pour any unused emulsion back into its bottle and store it in the fridge. Allow the screen to dry in a flat position in the darkened room and wash out the squeegee. To speed up the drying process you can use a hairdryer on a cool setting.

4. Expose the screen

Once the printing screen is thoroughly dry place the acetate onto the outside of the screen, so that the image is reversed, and secure the edges with sticky tape. Carefully place the sheet of glass on top of the acetate – the weight of the glass will ensure that the image on the acetate is in direct contact with the printing screen (otherwise the image will not develop correctly). Position the anglepoise lamp 30cm (12in) directly above the image and expose the printing screen to the light of the lamp for 1 hour. **(b)**

5. Wash out the image

Lift off the glass and gently peel away the acetate from the screen. Use a shower attachment over a bath to wash away the areas of photo emulsion that form the image with

lukewarm water – do not use hot water! The image will be slightly yellow. It might take a little time to wash away the emulsion, but gentle persistence and circular movements with a stencil brush will eventually reveal the image. **(c)** Allow the screen to dry, then paint out any holes in the screen with screen-filler/block using a medium paintbrush.

6. Prepare the screen for printing

Using masking tape, mask off a border along each side of the image to prevent ink seepage when printing (see step 5, page 108). Do the same to the other side of the screen.

7. Prepare to print

Tape a large sheet of newsprint to your work surface. Lay the scarf onto an A3 sheet of newsprint and fold the top half of the scarf out of the way. Create registration marks by marking out the bottom half of the scarf on the newsprint with a marker pen. Then lay the screen face-down onto the scarf so that the image is positioned 2.5–5cm (1–2in) from the bottom and the left-hand edge of the scarf and mark out the screen's edges on the newsprint.

8. Take a proof print

It is worth taking a proof print on cartridge paper first to check that everything is printing correctly. Once you have created registration marks for printing, remove the scarf and replace it with a sheet of paper. Take a proof print by

following the printing instructions in step 9. Once you are happy with the image, tape the bottom half of the scarf into place on the newsprint and print your scarf.

9. Print the scarf

Spoon ink onto the inside of the printing screen, 2.5cm (1in) above the top of the image so that it creates a rectangular pool about 2.5cm (1in) deep and as wide as the width of the image. Position the squeegee behind the ink and pull it towards you in one action, pulling the ink over the design. **(d)** The ink will print right through the scarf onto the newsprint; if possible, enlist an extra pair of hands to place a fresh sheet of newsprint in the printing area while you lift the printed end of the scarf and the used newsprint and swivel it around to the other side of the work surface. Place the unprinted end of the scarf on the fresh newsprint and print this as described above. (Draping the printed scarf over your arm is the best way of moving it if there isn't anyone around to help.) Allow the printed scarf to dry, then heat-set the ink with a warm iron (see page 11).

10. Clean up

To clean the frame, run water into the bottom of the bath to dilute any chemicals and sit the frame a little higher in the bath so that it is not in contact with the water. Follow the manufacturer's instructions for cleaning the screen.

LITHOGRAPHY

Of all the printmaking processes, lithography was a technique I always wanted to be able to do at home but thought that it would be impossible without the proper equipment and chemicals. It was a process that I found very exciting at college because it reproduces the subtlety of a crayon drawing in print. Lithography exploits the fact that oil and water do not mix; there is no carving involved, just direct drawing and painting onto a prepared surface. Because the drawn image is oily, it attracts ink to its surface and repels water so that you can print from it. Of all the print processes lithography is the closest to natural drawing and painting.

Artist and teacher of drawing/engraving Émilie Aizier-Brouard, along with intaglio press manufacturer Gary Bruno-Thibeau, have researched the use of aluminium foil and cola to formulate "kitchen lithography" – with some exciting results. I have tried out their process and made some adjustments and alterations for the home printmaker – what follows is my take.

CREATING A LITHO PLATE

LITHO PLATE KIT

Scissors	5H pencil
Extra-strong smooth aluminium foil	Korns Litho pencil no. 1 (you can use oil crayon but litho crayon gives a finer, better line)
Millboard (use the card from the back of a sketchpad or reinforced envelope, or purchase online in sheets)	A jar of cold water
Newsprint	100% olive-oil soap, for large flat areas of colour (available in health-food shops)
Sticky tape	A size 8 pointed, round paintbrush
Tracing paper	Hairdryer with a cool setting
2B pencil	

METHOD

1. Create the litho plate

Cut a strip of aluminium foil to a size two-and-a-half times the size of your millboard. You will be using the dull, inner side of the foil not the bright, shiny side; do not touch the dull, inner side of the foil. Lay the aluminium foil, dull-side down, onto a sheet of newsprint. Position the millboard in the centre of the foil and wrap the board up, securing the foil's edges with sticky tape positioned in the middle and at both ends of the board. **(a)** Make sure that the edges of the folded foil and exposed card are sealed with tape to avoid water penetration.

2. Transfer the image onto the litho plate

Traditionally artists draw freehand onto litho plates, which you can, of course, do as litho plates are great for sketching on. I have found, though, that it is easier to draw out a specific image when I have an outline to use as a guide. This technique lets you transfer the outline of an image onto the plate.

Trace your image onto tracing paper using a 2B pencil (see page 10). Carefully turn the litho plate over, taking care not to touch the front surface. Flip your traced image over and place it onto the foil plate, securing the edges onto the work surface with tape so that it doesn't move. The image you see is reversed but the final image will print the correct way round. Using a 5H pencil, draw over the image – this will create indentation lines in the foil that will be used as a guide for drawing the image. **(b)**

3. Draw the image on the litho plate.

Remove the tracing paper and, using a litho pencil, draw out the image. Try not to lean on or touch the surface of the foil, as grease can easily become part of the printed image. The places where the litho pencil leaves a dark line will become the printed image, so it is important to go over any weak lines.

To create large areas of flat colour, put a little water onto the bar of soap, mix around with a paintbrush until the surface is creamy and paint this onto the template areas of the plate. When you have finished this dry the plate with a hairdryer on a cool setting.

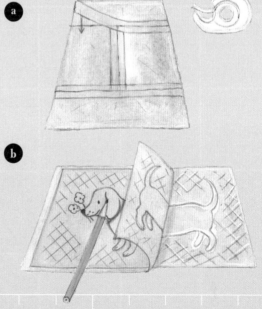

a

b

LITTLE DOG CARD
one-colour lithography

One of my trademark images is my little sausage dog. I love Dachshunds, and this character is based on my dear friend's little dog Nougat.

As an introduction to lithography, I wanted to keep the first project as simple as possible and quite traditional. I really admire the artist Pierre Bonnard's lithographic drawings; there is something so simple and charming about them. This little card is a lithographic drawing created using a lithographic pencil and printed in a traditional brown colour.

LEVEL
Intermediate

TEMPLATES
Little dog (see inside front cover), enlarged by 200%

YOU WILL NEED

Litho plate kit (see page 122), with millboard cut to 24 x 15cm (9½ x 6in)

Old or cheap plastic tablecloth

Access to water and a sink or washing-up bowl

Newspaper

Rapeseed oil

Kitchen paper

2 plastic or foil tray containers

2 different-coloured super-absorbent cellulose sponges (often sold in supermarkets in packs of 3)

Plastic bag

Old chopping mat or a piece of bevel-edged glass, for rolling out paint

2cm (¾in) flat paintbrush or other large, soft paintbrush

Gum arabic

Disposable or rubber gloves

Bottle of cola (which must contain phosphoric acid)

Oil paint or traditional oil-based printing inks – colour of your choice. (You may want to buy just one colour for use in this project. Alternatively, if you'd like to try your hand at the next litho-printing project too – Little fishes print, see page 128 – you could buy crimson, blue, yellow, black and white, mix your own colour, and reuse the colours for the next project. You can also buy a starter pack of five to six small tubes of basic oil paint very reasonably.)

Hog-hair paintbrush, for mixing paint

Thickened linseed oil – needed if your paints are stiff, as it helps to improve the flow of paint

Foam roller

Protective goggles

Light-weight cartridge paper or other smooth paper cut to approx. 2.5cm (1in) larger than your litho plate

Large, smooth, heavy, round pebble, or wooden spoon

Washing-up liquid

METHOD

1. Prepare the template and the litho plate

Enlarge the Little dog template on the inside front cover, then trace the image onto tracing paper using a 2B pencil (see page 10). **(a)** Create your litho plate and transfer the image as described on page 122.

2. Prepare the processing and printing areas

Because lithography uses oil paint, which is not water soluble, you should protect your work surface with an old or cheap plastic tablecloth. Work in a well-ventilated space with access to water and a sink. It is a good idea to divide your workspace into two areas. Each area needs several sheets of newspaper: one area will be for processing and "rolling up" your plate and the other area will be for printing. The processing area should contain a bottle of rapeseed oil, kitchen paper, two plastic or foil tray containers filled with cold water, two different-coloured cellulose sponges (one will be the clean sponge,

the other will be the rolling-up sponge), a plastic bag for the disposal of used paper, an old chopping mat or a piece of bevel-edged glass for rolling out paint, a large soft paintbrush and a bottle of gum arabic.

3. Process the litho plate

It is important to wear disposable or rubber gloves when processing and rolling up your litho plate. When you are satisfied with your drawing, hold your litho plate over the

b

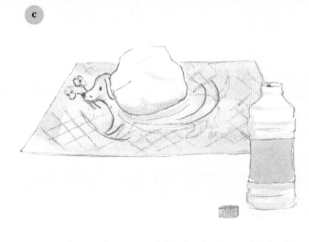

c

sink or washing-up bowl. Pour cola over the whole surface of the plate to etch your plate **(b)**. You will see that the drawing will fizz with bubbles. To ensure a good etch, hold the litho plate level to keep the cola on the surface for a few seconds. Rinse off the cola with cold water (warm water would melt the crayon and ruin your picture!) then place the litho plate onto a sheet of newspaper in your processing area. Lay a sheet of kitchen paper on top of the litho plate, and pat this very gently (do not rub it as this will disturb the drawing). Remove the damp kitchen paper. Pour a few drops of rapeseed oil onto the plate and wipe over the plate gently with kitchen paper **(c)**. Use a fresh piece of kitchen paper to gently wipe the plate clean. Refresh the newspaper under the litho plate. With the clean, damp sponge squeeze a little cold water over the litho plate, then wring out the sponge and gently wipe it over the plate: the aim is to have a thin film of water on the plate (this will prevent the paint from adhering to any areas of the plate other than the oily litho drawing).

4. Roll up the plate

Mix up or squeeze out your chosen paint colour onto an old chopping mat or a piece of bevel-edged glass, adding a little thickened linseed oil to improve the flow of the paint if necessary. Roll the foam roller in the paint, and make sure that it is evenly covered with paint (but not sticky and over-laden) by rolling it out onto a clear area on the mat or

glass – it should make a wispy sound as you roll it. Make sure that the plate is still damp by wiping over it with the damp rolling-up sponge before rolling up with paint, as this will prevent areas other than the drawing from taking up all the paint. Gently roll the roller over the areas of the image where you can see the thin film of water being repelled on the plate. When you roll paint onto the litho plate, it is important that you roll lightly, lifting the roller after each roll. You will notice that the drawn image will start to pick up the paint. After a couple of rolls of the roller, wipe over the plate again with the damp rolling-up sponge; this will help to clean off any scum on the plate and transfer the paint into the drawn areas of the plate **(d)**.

5. Add the gum arabic to the litho plate

When you are satisfied with the rolled-up image, add the gum arabic to the litho plate. Working in a well-ventilated area and wearing protective goggles and disposable or rubber gloves, pour ½ teaspoonful of gum arabic onto the plate and gently paint this over the whole plate with the large, soft paintbrush. **(e)** The gum arabic will make the undrawn areas of the plate even less attracted to oil paint, giving you a cleaner, more reliable image. Allow the plate to dry – to speed up the process you can dry your plate with a hairdryer on a cool setting. Once the litho plate is dry, rinse it under a cold tap, shake off the excess water and transfer it to fresh newspaper in the rolling-up area.

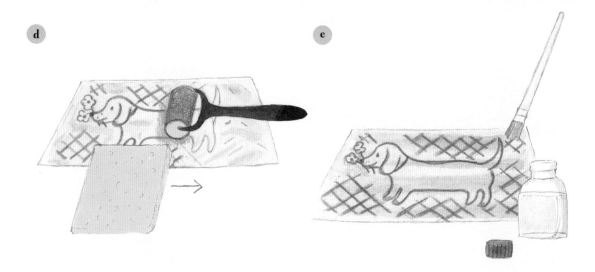

d   e

Wipe over the plate again with the damp rolling-up sponge (it is important to immerse the sponge in clean water and squeeze it out occasionally throughout the rolling-up process to help keep it relatively clean), roll up the image with paint again, gently wiping off any scum on the plate with the damp sponge. When you are happy with the rolled-up image, transfer the plate to your printing area.

6. Print the image

With clean hands, position a sheet of cartridge paper centrally on top of the printing plate. Smooth the back of the paper with the palm of your hand, taking care not to move it – I found that the slight dampness of the plate held the paper in place, but the plate mustn't be so wet that the paper disintegrates during the printing process. Using the pebble or the back of a wooden spoon, make circular movements over the whole surface of the paper. Carefully remove the print and allow it to dry – because you are using oil paint, this will take about 48 hours.

7. Continue printing

You will notice, as you continue to roll up and print more prints, that the image will become stronger. Transfer the litho plate to the rolling-up area, again wipe over the plate with the damp rolling-up sponge. You will find that the paint will be attracted to the drawn image. Repeat the rolling-up and printing process. You should be able

to print off 20 prints, or more. If you find that your drawing keeps scumming up, roll up the plate with paint and wipe it as if you were going to print, pour cola over the plate to etch it again, rinse the plate and apply a teaspoon of gum arabic over it and allow it to dry. When the plate is dry, rinse off the gum arabic with cold water and roll up the litho plate as before.

8. Clean up

To clean up, make sure that you wear rubber gloves. I use a little rapeseed oil poured onto the rolling-up surface. Roll the roller in this to dilute the oil paint and wipe the surface clean with kitchen paper. Clean the roller, brush, sponges and mat or glass separately using neat washing-up liquid and hot soapy water – you will need to wash the sponge roller several times to get it clean. Dry with kitchen paper. Strip the aluminium foil off the printing plate and discard this along with the newspaper, but keep the millboard for making new plates. Clean off any scum in your sink with cream cleaner.

LITTLE FISHES PRINT

three-colour lithography

This three-colour lithograph shows how effective home lithographic printing can be. I love the softness of the colours, the crayon line and large, flat areas of paint, which I have created using olive-oil soap.

Printing three colours requires some patience because you have to print the light colours first followed by the darker colours. I find this quite hard, as I am always impatient to see how the finished image is going to turn out!

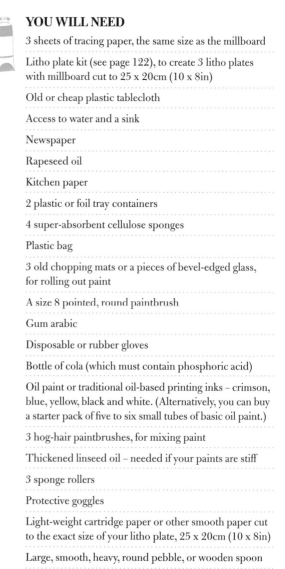

YOU WILL NEED

3 sheets of tracing paper, the same size as the millboard

Litho plate kit (see page 122), to create 3 litho plates with millboard cut to 25 x 20cm (10 x 8in)

Old or cheap plastic tablecloth

Access to water and a sink

Newspaper

Rapeseed oil

Kitchen paper

2 plastic or foil tray containers

4 super-absorbent cellulose sponges

Plastic bag

3 old chopping mats or a pieces of bevel-edged glass, for rolling out paint

A size 8 pointed, round paintbrush

Gum arabic

Disposable or rubber gloves

Bottle of cola (which must contain phosphoric acid)

Oil paint or traditional oil-based printing inks – crimson, blue, yellow, black and white. (Alternatively, you can buy a starter pack of five to six small tubes of basic oil paint.)

3 hog-hair paintbrushes, for mixing paint

Thickened linseed oil – needed if your paints are stiff

3 sponge rollers

Protective goggles

Light-weight cartridge paper or other smooth paper cut to the exact size of your litho plate, 25 x 20cm (10 x 8in)

Large, smooth, heavy, round pebble, or wooden spoon

Washing-up liquid

LEVEL

Difficult

TEMPLATES

Little fishes (see page 132), enlarged by 200%

METHOD

1. Prepare the templates

Enlarge the Little fishes template on page 132, then trace each of the 3 colour separations onto a separate sheet of tracing paper with a 2B pencil, lining up the edge of each sheet with the border of the template in each instance.

2. Create the litho plates

Prepare 3 litho plates as described on page 122. Lining up the edges of the tracing paper with the edges of the plates, trace each separation onto a separate plate and write firmly through the tracing paper in the right-hand corner of the plate the first letter of each plate colour to avoid confusion when printing, and to indicate which way up the plate should be. For plates 1 and 3, draw out the image with the litho pencil. For plate 2, create the large area of flat colour by putting a little water onto the bar of soap, mixing around with a paintbrush until the surface is creamy, and painting this onto the template areas of the plate. **(a)** When you have finished, dry plate 2 with a hairdryer on a cool setting.

3. Prepare the processing and printing areas

Prepare your processing and printing areas as described in step 2 on page 125.

4. Mix the paint colours

Mix up and roll out the paint colours onto old chopping mats or pieces of bevel-edged glass, adding a little thickened linseed oil to improve the flow of the paint if necessary. The colours I mixed are:

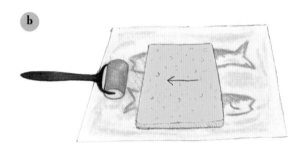

Plate 1 – pale blue from blue, white and a little yellow
Plate 2 – pink from crimson, white and a little yellow
Plate 3 – medium grey from blue, black and white

5. Process the litho plates

Wear disposable or rubber gloves when processing and rolling up the litho plates, and protective goggles when using gum arabic. Process the plates one at a time by etching them with cola, loading them up with paint, applying a coating of gum arabic and allowing them to dry – as described in detail in steps 3–5 on pages 125–127.

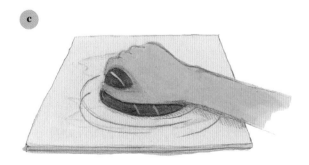

Plates in order of printing

Plate 1

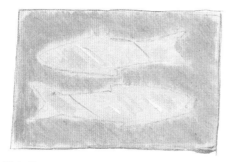

Plate 2

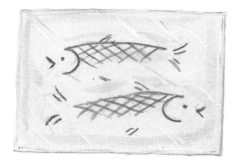

Plate 3

6. Print plate 1

Rinse plate 1 (the pale blue fishes) under cold water, shake off any excess water from the plate and transfer it to fresh newspaper in the loading-up area. Make sure that the plate is still damp by wiping over it with the clean, damp sponge before rolling up with paint. Roll up the image with pale blue paint, gently wiping off any scum with the damp rolling-up sponge. **(b)** When you are happy with the image, transfer this to your printing area. Draw an arrow on the back of the piece of printing paper so that you know which way up the paper should be. With clean hands, position a sheet of cartridge paper on top of the plate so that it is lined up with all four edges of the plate. Smooth the back of the paper with the palm of your hand, taking care not to move it. Using a pebble or the back of a wooden spoon, make circular movements over the whole surface of the paper **(c)**, then carefully remove the print. Transfer the plate to the loading-up area, again wipe over the plate with a damp sponge and repeat the loading-up and printing process. You should be able to print off 20 prints, or more.

7. Print plate 2

Repeat step 6 with plate 2 (the pink background colour). Don't be afraid to be firm when wiping the scum off the plate: if you find that the loaded-up surface is a little smeared when wiping it, just make sure that it is damp and carefully roll over the loaded-up areas again. When the image is ready to print, place the plate in the printing area. Take a print and position it on top of plate 2, making sure that the plate and paper are the right way up and lined up with the edges of the plate, and print the image. Repeat the process of loading up with paint and printing to print this second colour on all of the prints.

8. Print plate 3 and clean up

Repeat step 6 with plate 3 (the medium grey fish details) and allow the final prints to dry for 48 hours before framing. Clean up your workspace and equipment as described in step 8 on page 127.

TEMPLATES

Pear 1 (page 72)

Pear 2 (page 72)

 Little fishes
Plate 1 (page 128)

Little fishes
Plate 2 (page 128)

 Little fishes
Plate 3 (page 128)

Teapot (page 82)

Flying bird (page 62)

Red separation

Blue separation

Black separation

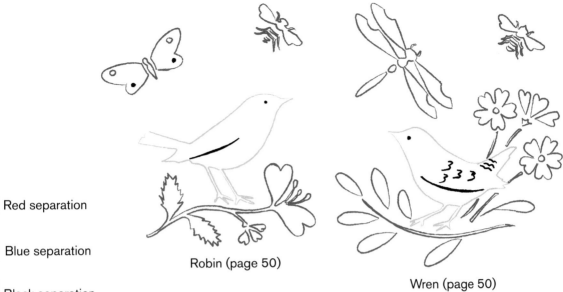

Robin (page 50)

Wren (page 50)

Songthrush (page 50)

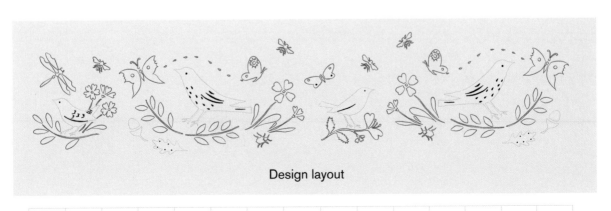

Design layout

Bluebird (page 102)

Flower guide

Butterfly charmer (page 116)

Summer flowers (page 47)

Green separation

Red separation

Blue separation

White separation

Purple separation

Black separation

Yellow separation

Companion cat (page 106)

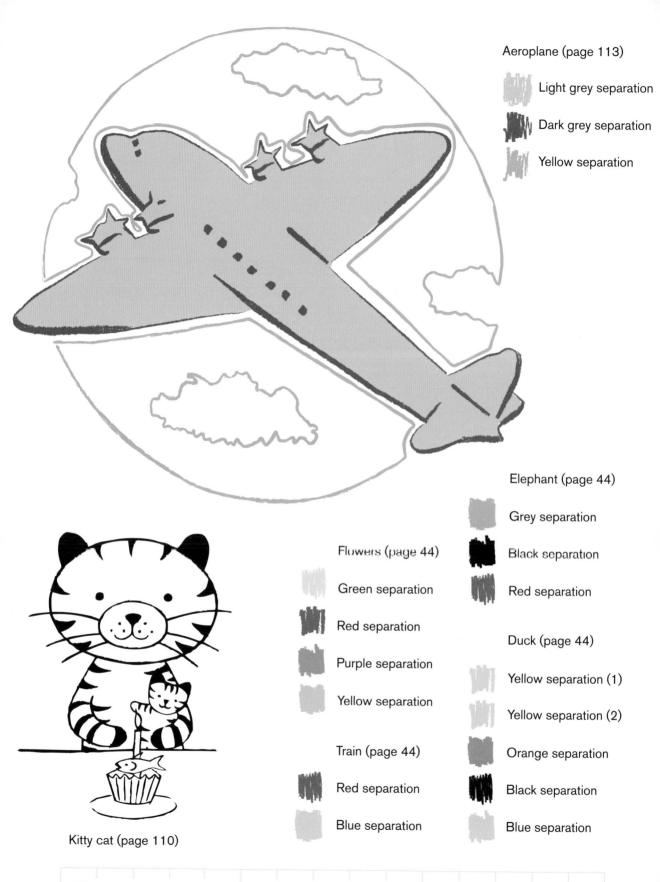

Aeroplane (page 113)

Light grey separation

Dark grey separation

Yellow separation

Elephant (page 44)

Grey separation

Black separation

Red separation

Flowers (page 44)

Green separation

Red separation

Purple separation

Yellow separation

Duck (page 44)

Yellow separation (1)

Yellow separation (2)

Orange separation

Black separation

Train (page 44)

Red separation

Blue separation

Blue separation

Kitty cat (page 110)

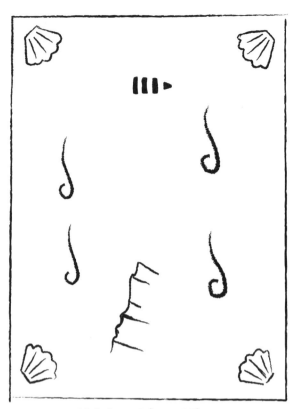

Little boat 1 (page 85)

Little boat 2 (page 85)

Topiary garden (page 91)

GLOSSARY

Acrylic paint A versatile water-based paint that is water-resistant when dry.

Acrylic textile medium A clear liquid that, when mixed with acrylic paint, enables the paint to remain "open" or wet on a screen-printing screen and colourfast when printed on fabric.

Block-printing A printing method that uses a relief surface design mounted onto a wooden block, which is then applied with ink and stamped onto fabric or paper.

Block-printing medium Used with acrylic paint to make relief-printing ink.

Brayer A rubber hand-roller used to transfer ink onto a printing surface or to apply even pressure to the back of the surface being printed.

Carrageenan A seaweed extract, also known as *Chrondus crispus* (Irish moss) used as a thickener that can be mixed with water to create a gel or "size", a viscous solution on which inks can float and be manipulated.

Cartridge paper High-quality, heavy, smooth, versatile paper often used for drawing.

Cutting mat Used to protect work surfaces and prevent premature blunting of a scalpel (X-Acto knife) or craft knife blade.

De-ionised water Water that is filtered to remove impurities.

Gelatine Used in the food industry as a gelling agent. When dissolved in water in the right proportions it makes a firm, gelatinous surface.

Gum arabic Used in lithography to make undrawn areas of a litho plate less attracted to oil/ink.

Repositional book-covering film Wipeable, self-adhesive clear film that can be used as a mask on fabric.

Hog-hair brush A strong, flexible-bristled brush that can move and manipulate thick paint.

Lino-cut A relief surface created by carving out a design with lino-cutting tools.

Lino-cutting tools Used to cut or carve a relief surface, traditionally out of lino, although other materials can be used such as softcut printing blocks.

Lithography A printing technique where an image is drawn directly onto a flat metal or stone surface. The surface, or litho plate, is then processed so that the drawn areas attract oil-based ink that can be printed from.

Millboard The dense, smooth, grey board found at the back of sketchbooks. Can be bought in sheets.

Marbling A process of floating inks upon "size" to create patterns, which are then transferred to paper.

Mask/stencil film Adhesive low-tack transparent film.

Matrix A design created on a printing plate or block which can be used to print from several times.

Mono-printing A process where a printable surface is painted on in various ways to create an image. The image is transferred to paper by bringing paper into contact with the surface and applying pressure. This is often referred to as a printed painting.

Newsprint Low-cost, off-white absorbent paper made from recycled waste fibres used to print newspapers.

Organza (polyester) A thin, lightweight, sheer plain-weave fabric.

Photo emulsion A light-sensitive coating on a screen that can be exposed with a half-tone photograph or fine-lined drawing to create a printable image.

Pipette Used to hold and release liquid in a measured way.

Pointed round brush Made from either synthetic or natural fibre, this type of brush has a good paint-carrying capacity and can create both wide and fine brush strokes.

Ponge 5 silk A weight of silk fabric.

Printing plate/block The means of transferring an image to paper or fabric.

Quickprint foam/polystyrene Used in basic relief-printing, a surface that can be easily imprinted with a firm pencil or other instrument to create a relief surface design.

Quilting hoop A round frame used in quilting and embroidery to stretch fabric taut.

Relief-printing A raised surface with recesses, often created out of a flat surface by cutting/carving an image to create areas that remain free of printing ink. The recesses show white when the image is printed.

Scalpel (X-Acto knife) A sharp small-bladed knife with interchangeable blades used for precision cutting.

Screen drawing fluid Used to create a positive image on a screen-printing screen.

Screen-filler/block Used to block out areas of an image that you do not wish to print on a screen.

Screen-printing A method of printing where a frame is covered in a screen mesh, which is then blocked out with either stencils or screen-filler/block to create an image. Ink is passed over the screen and, where the screen is exposed, an image is printed.

Size (1) The substance that is used as a protective sealant on fabric surfaces to keep them smooth and crease-free. (2) The suspension solution that the paint floats upon in a marbling bath.

Sponge roller An absorbent roller used to transfer paint onto a printing surface.

Stencil-printing A process in which an image is built up by printing through various colour-separated (reusable) stencils.

Stretched canvas A wooden frame over which plain canvas has been stretched and attached.

Squeegee A rubber or plastic blade which can move ink across a surface in a controlled way.

Tracing paper A translucent paper.

Printmaking Supplies (UK)

Artesaver
www.artesaver.co.uk

George Weil & Sons Ltd
Old Portsmouth Road
Guildford
Surrey GU3 1LZ
+44 (0) 1483 565800
www.georgeweil.com

Great Art
www.greatart.co.uk

Intaglio Printmaker
9 Playhouse Court
62 Southwark Bridge Road
London SE1 0AT
+44 (0)20 7928 2633
www.intaglioprintmaker.com

T N Lawrence & Son Ltd
208 Portland Road
Hove
East Sussex BN3 5QT
+44 (0)1273 260280
www.lawrence.co.uk

Printmaking Supplies (US)

McClain's Printmaking Supplies
www.imcclains.com

Speedball
www.speedballart.com

Art materials (UK)

Chromos Art Supplies
www.chromosart.co.uk

Hobbycraft *(shops nationwide)*
www.hobbycraft.co.uk

Jacksons Art Supplies Ltd
1 Farleigh Place
London N16 7SX
+44 (0)844 499 8430
www.jacksonsart.com

London Graphic Centre
16–18 Shelton Street
London WC2H 9JL
+44 (0)20 7759 4500
www.londongraphics.co.uk

M Saltmarsh
32 Monson Road
Tunbridge Wells
Kent TN1 1LU
+44 (0)1892 527512
www.msaltmarsh.com

The Works *(shops nationwide)*
www.theworks.co.uk

Art materials (US)

A C Moore Arts & Crafts
www.acmoore.com

Dick Blick Art Materials
www.dickblick.com

Hobby Lobby
www.hobbylobby.com

Jo-Ann Fabric and Craft Stores
www.joann.com

Michaels
www.michaels.com

Paper (UK)

Economy of Brighton
Unit 1 Westergate Business Park
Westergate Road
Brighton BN2 4QN
+44 (0)1273 682831
www.economyofbrighton.co.uk

John Purcell Paper
*(wholesaler of artists' papers sold
in packs of 25 upwards)*
15 Rumsey Road
London SW9 0TR
+44 (0)20 7737 5199
www.johnpurcell.net

Poundland *(shops nationwide)*
www.poundland.co.uk

Paper (US)

Hollander's
www.hollanders.com

Kate's Paperie
www.katespaperie.com

Paper Source
www.paper-source.com

Fabrics (UK)

Ada & Ina
www.linenfabrics.co.uk

Depotex
16 Fisher Street
Lewes BN7 2DG
+44 (0)1273 487956

Dunelm Mill *(shops nationwide)*
www.dunelm-mill.com

Ikea
www.ikea.com/gb/en/

John Lewis
Oxford Street
London W1A 1EX
(and shops nationwide)
08456 049049 (from the UK)
+44 (0)1698 545454

The Sewing Room
101 High Street
West Malling
Kent ME19 6NA
+44 (0)1732 848936

Wolfin textiles
www.wolfintextiles.co.uk

World of Sewing
56–64 Camden Road
Tunbridge Wells
Kent TN1 2QP
+44 (0)1892 533188
www.worldofsewing.com

Other materials (UK)

Argos
www.argos.co.uk

eBay
www.ebay.co.uk

Tiger
www.tigerstores.co.uk

Wickes
www.wickes.co.uk

Wilkinson
www.wilkinsonplus.com

INDEX

A

acrylic retarder liquid 10
acrylic textile medium 10
aeroplane T-shirt 113–15, 136
Aizier-Brouard, Émilie 121
  animal motifs
    children's birthday cards 44–6, 136–7
    children's party invitations 110–12,
     136
    companion cat cushion 106–9, 135
    little dog card 124–7
    little fishes print 128–31, 132
autumn tablecloth 72–3, 132

B

bags
  bluebird drawstring bag 102–5, 134
  love heart tote bag 28–30
  summer flowers tote bag 47–9, 135
bird motifs
  bird nest wall art 20–3
  children's party invitations 110–12,
   136
  flying bird cushion 62–4
  flying bird mobile 24–7
  garden birds lampshade 50–3, 133
  songthrush card 88–90
birthday cards 44–6, 136–7
block-printing 58
  adding details to motifs 58
  country house table linen 65–7
  cutting out foam 58
  flying bird cushion 62–4
  making block 58
  making mount 58
  patterned wrapping paper & tags 60–1
  tracing and transferring design 58
bluebird drawstring bag 102–5, 134
boat picture 85–7, 138
bookmarks 17–19
botanical curtain 74–6
bowls, folk art 54–5
brayers 9
Bruno-Thibeau, Gary 121
bubble wrap 27
butterfly motifs
  butterfly-charmer scarf 116–19, 134
  dragon & butterfly drawer papers
   69–71
  vibrant butterfly cards 37–9

C

cards
  children's birthday cards 44–6, 136–7
  little dog card 124–7
  songthrush card 88–90
  teatime greetings card 82–4, 132
  vibrant butterfly cards 37–9
children's birthday cards 44–6, 136–7
children's party invitations 110–12,
  136
china bowls, folk art 54–5
clothing 8
collage
  bird nest wall art 20–3
  home sweet home print 31–3
companion cat cushion 106–9, 135
country house table linen 65–7
cross-hatching 26
curtain, botanical 74–6
cushions
  companion cat cushion 106–9, 135
  flying bird cushion 62–4
cutting mats 8

D

decorative papers 41
drawer papers, dragonfly & butterfly
  69–71
drawing fluid
  children's party invitations 110–12,
   136
  companion cat cushion 106–9, 135
drawstring bag, bluebird 102–5, 134
dry-brush techniques
  garden birds lampshade 50–3, 133

E

envelopes 80–1
equipment 8–9, 96
etching 13

F

fabric 11
  heat-setting printed image onto
   fabric 11
  if something goes wrong 11
  preparation of fabric 11
fabric-printing 57
  aeroplane T-shirt 113–15, 136
  autumn tablecloth 72–3, 132
  bluebird drawstring bag 102–5, 134
  botanical curtain 74–6
  companion cat cushion 106–9, 135
  country house table linen 65–7
  feather table runner 77–9
  flying bird cushion 62–4
  hen tea towel 99–101
  love heart tote bag 28–30
  summer flowers tote bag 47–9, 135
fabric screen-printing ink 10
feather table runner 77–9
floral notebooks & bookmarks 17–19
flying bird cushion 62–4
flying bird mobile 24–7
foam rollers 9
folk art bowls 54

G

garden birds lampshade 50–3, 133
gelatine 14
  preparing for printing 14
  setting 14
  using again 14
ghost prints 18
  floral notebooks & bookmarks 17–19
  love heart tote bag 28–30

H

hen tea towel 99–101
home sweet home print 31–3

I

invitations 110–12, 136

J

jelly-printing 13
  bird nest wall art 20–3
  bubble wrap 27
  creating surface 14
  cross-hatching 26
  floral notebooks & bookmarks
   17–19
  flying bird mobile 24–7
  home sweet home print 31–3
  horizontal streaks 26
  lace 26–7, 31
  love heart tote bag 28–30
  registration marks 22
  taking silhouette print 18, 31
  two-colour variation 19

K

kitchen lithography 121
kitchenware and utensils 9

L

lace 26–7, 31
lampshade, garden birds 50–3, 133
layers
  bird nest wall art 20–3
letterheads, envelopes & tags 80–1

lino-cutting 68
  autumn tablecloth 72–3, 132
  dragonfly & butterfly drawer papers
    69–71
  letterheads, envelopes & tags 80–1
  little boat picture 85–7, 138
  teatime greetings card 82–4, 132
lithography 121
  creating litho plate 122
  drawing image on litho plate 122
  little dog card 124–7
  little fishes print 128–31, 132
  transferring image onto litho
    plate 122
little boat picture 85–7, 138
little dog card 124–7
little fishes print 128–31, 132

M
manipulated paint 27
  bird nest wall art 20–3
marbling 13, 34
  creating feathered marbling surface 41
  making marbling comb 36
  mixing paint colours 36
  preparing marbling bath 36
  preparing marbling inks 36
  preparing workspace 36
  pretty decorative papers 41
  vibrant butterfly cards 37–9
materials 9–10
mobile, flying bird 24–7
  making the mobile 27
mono-printing 13
  bird nest wall art 20–3
  floral notebooks & bookmarks
    17–19
  flying bird mobile 24–7
  home sweet home print 31–3
  love heart tote bag 28–30
  vibrant butterfly cards 37–9

N
newsprint 10
notebooks 17–19

P
paint 9–10, 96
paintbrushes 9
paper 10
papers, decorative 41
party invitations 110–12, 136
pencils 8–9
photo-emulsion screen-printing

butterfly-charmer scarf 116–19, 134
photocopy paper 10
polystyrene printing
  songthrush card 88–90
  topiary garden print 91–3, 138–9
potato-printing
  autumn tablecloth 72–3, 132
  dragonfly & butterfly drawer papers
    69–71

Q
quilting hoop screen-printing
  children's party invitations 110–12,
    136

R
relief-printing 57
  botanical curtain 74–6
  feather table runner 77–9
  letterheads, envelopes & tags 80–1
rollers 9
rubber stamps, home-made 80
ruler, metal 8

S
scalpels 8
scarf, butterfly-charmer 116–19, 134
screen-printing 95
  aeroplane T-shirt 113–15, 136
  before starting 98
  bluebird drawstring bag 102–5, 134
  butterfly-charmer scarf 116–19, 134
  checking and finishing frame 98
  children's party invitations 110–12,
    136
  companion cat cushion 106–9, 135
  equipment and paint 96
  hen tea towel 99–101
  home-made printing screen 96
  preparing organza 98
  removing canvas from frame 98
  stapling organza to frame 98
songthrush card 88
Speedy-Carve 82, 85
sponge rollers 9
stencil-printing 43
  bluebird drawstring bag 102–5, 134
  children's birthday cards 44–6,
    136–7
  cutting stencils 44–5
  folk art bowls 54–5
  garden birds lampshade 50–3, 133
  summer flowers tote bag 47–9, 135
summer flowers tote bag 47–9, 135

T
T-shirt, aeroplane 113–15, 136
tablecloth, autumn 72–3, 132
table linen, country house 65–7
runner, feather 77–9
tea towel, hen 99–101
teatime greetings card 82–4, 132
templates
  aeroplane T-shirt 136
  autumn tablecloth 132
  bluebird drawstring bag 134
  butterfly charmer 134
  children's birthday cards 136–7
  children's party invitations 136
  companion cat cushion 135
  garden birds lampshade 133
  little boat picture 138
  little fishes print 132
  summer flowers tote bag 135
  teatime greetings card 132
  topiary garden print 138–9
three-colour lithography
  little fishes print 128–31, 132
three-colour screen-printing
  aeroplane T-shirt 113–15, 136
topiary garden print 91–3, 138–9
tote bag, love heart 28–30
tote bag, summer flowers 47–9, 135
tracing and transferring images 10
tracing paper 10
two-colour block-printing
  country house table linen 65–7
two-colour lino-cutting
  little boat picture 85–7, 138
two-colour relief-printing
  botanical curtain 74–6

U
U cutters 68, 84

V
V cutters 68, 83, 86

W
wall art
  bird nest 20–3
  home sweet home print 31–3
  little boat picture 85–7, 138
  little fishes print 128–31, 132
  topiary garden print 91–3, 138–9
wax resist
  bluebird drawstring bag 102–5, 134
workspaces 8
wrapping paper & tags 60–1

ACKNOWLEDGEMENTS

A very special thanks to Alison, the publisher, who saw the idea in my Christmas card.
Thank you for having faith in me and for giving me the creative freedom to make this book.

To Jonathan, for thinking of me.

A special thanks to my editor, Leanne, for her kind help and support, and to Katy, for making sure that everything made sense.
To Juliette, Anita and Abi, for putting together such a beautifully designed book. To Yuki, for the gorgeous photographs;
to Kim, for all her help on the shoot; and to Cynthia, who introduced me to the stylist's visual narrative!

A special thanks to my dear friend Karen, who very kindly lent us her beautiful house for part of the shoot.

A very special thanks to my wonderful husband, Llewellyn, for his unending support, love and encouragement. And to my dear
children, Esme and Sam, for all their fantastic help, creativity, humour and patience – you make my days so special!

Finally, thanks to Maidstone College of Art, where the magic began!

ABOUT THE AUTHOR

Elizabeth Harbour is an illustrator, designer and printmaker. She has a BA in illustration
from Maidstone College of Art and an MA from the Royal College of Art. She has worked
in the fields of children's book illustration, book jacket design, magazine editorial, greetings
cards, gift wrap, food packaging, decorative maps, promotional leaflets and advertising, and
has taught in various art colleges. She lives in rural Kent with her husband and two children.
For the last two years Elizabeth has been running an art class called "Art For Enjoyment"
alongside her commercial work, and producing her own prints to sell in galleries and shops
in the UK. Visit her website for more information: www.elizabethharbour.co.uk

A NOTE FROM THE AUTHOR

If you have enjoyed the projects in this book, I hope that you take the
processes further to create your own works of art! And if you are able to,
seek out a local print studio where you can expand your print experience.